DATE DUE

OC 2 9 '96			
~~OC 2 1 '98~~			

DEMCO 38-296

TELECOMMUTING

A Manager's Guide to Flexible Work Arrangements

Joel Kugelmass

LEXINGTON BOOKS
An Imprint of The Free Press

NEW YORK   LONDON   TORONTO   SYDNEY   TOKYO   SINGAPORE

Library of Congress Cataloging-in-Publication Data

Kugelmass, Joel.
  Telecommuting : a manager's guide to flexible work arrangements / Joel Kugelmass.
    p.   cm.
  Includes bibliographical references and index.
  ISBN 0-02-917691-3
  1. Telecommuting. 2. Hours of labor, Flexible. I. Title.
HD2333.K84   1995
331.25—dc20   94-41403
                                                                          CIP

Lexington Books
An Imprint of The Free Press
A Division of Simon & Schuster Inc.
866 Third Avenue, New York, N. Y. 10022

Printed in the United States of America

printing number

1 2 3 4 5 6 7 8 9 10

To my son Joseph, and to his future

Contents

Preface

Flexibility seemed well on its way at my employer, the University of California, Davis. The Chancellor had just issued a ringing endorsement of telecommuting and flextime. The Telecommuting Task Force for which I worked launched the new flexibility policy with a series of lunch hour briefings attended by hundreds of employees. Their excitement was palpable, but so was their skepticism. Was this for real? Many openly doubted that their supervisors and managers would consent to the new policy. Their incredulity was well-founded.

When we put together a closed-door meeting for managers and supervisors, the large meeting room was again filled to capacity, but the mood was tense, and the questions were often hostile. When a supervisor declared her authority was being challenged, many nodded in agreement. Underneath the fractious questions were genuine anxieties. Their positions and hierarchies, often carefully developed over years, seemed threatened. One manager dubbed flexible work "an invitation to anarchy."

This book answers the apprehensions and misunderstandings with which many managers and supervisors view flexible work. It offers that wary supervisor who fears control will suffer evidence of the ways in which flexibility actually increases control through managing by objective. It encourages organizations to see how they can use flexible work arrangements to improve productivity and to reduce costs of space and skyrocketing absenteeism with only modest expenditures. It shows how management interested in a more effective and reliable work force can motivate flexibility programs. It demonstrates how telecommuting leverages existing technology and personnel investments. Rather than shying away from the risks of flexible work, this book suggests how they can be managed and minimized.

Flexible work discussions are shrouded in mythologies: flexible work is only for highly paid professionals, or it is only for low-paid clerical workers trying to solve child care problems, or it is an expensive excursion into the latest computer and communication technologies for the home office. These theories are debunked by the experiences of over a hundred companies and public agencies in every part of the United States and in Canada, Europe, and Japan. Flexibility can be applied to nearly every type of organization.

Flexible work is primarily a management strategy for organizations of every sector regardless of type of product, level of technology, or type of work force. Because per-employee costs of flexible work are low and are overwhelmed by cost-savings, both very large and very small organizations can apply flexible work; indeed, small-to-medium organizations may have the advantage of agility when they apply flexible work to increase productivity, improve recruitment, use space more efficiently, and provide better coverage to customer service functions. The downsized organization, making due with less and already changing the way it works, is similarly advantaged.

Is flexible work right for your organization? Almost certainly. Undertaken thoughtfully, flexible work can succeed in your organization as it has in natural gas companies, high-technology firms, police stations, advertising brokerages, universities, organizations of twenty-five employees, and those of 25,000. The critical factor of success is the manager, supervisor, and employee.

If I have even partly illuminated the issues of flexible work from a management point of view, it is because of good friends to this effort. I wish to thank the University of California, Davis, for assigning me rights to my report, "Telecommuting and Flextime for the UC Davis Administration." I am indebted to Patricia Mokhtarian, Assistant Professor of Civil Engineering at UC Davis, for her encouragement and for her unique help in researching flexible work issues. I thank my good friend Paul Rupert, a flexible work consultant with Work/Family Directions, and my wife, Lois, for believing in this book in the face of my hesitations. Finally, I give special thanks to my editor, Beth Anderson, who insisted on writing as purposeful and exact as possible.

I

Understanding Flexible Work

1

Working in a Changing World

In the upscale cafe in Sacramento, California, the entrepreneur across the table ignored his salad as the interview progressed. Instead, he relished describing the recent expansion of his architectural firm to Taipei, Taiwan. There, he emphasized, architects hire on for a tenth of the wages paid to comparable American professionals. "What they don't know," he allowed, "are our concepts and building codes." Architectural ideas are shipped from the Sacramento headquarters to Taiwanese employees by computer, fax, and occasional telephone calls. Digitized drawings, sent back by modem, get readily modified on computer screens to meet U.S. specifications.

I asked whether his architects here in California telecommute. He looked puzzled, then challenged. "You mean working from home? Oh yes, we're definitely thinking about that," he said, his discomfort evident. Turning to his meal with new-found devotion, he sought to deflect the obvious irony: Managing remote workers across an ocean is practical, indeed profitable, but managing remote workers across town is provocative, even threatening. The manager overseeing production thousands of miles and many time zones away gets uneasy when his staff wants to work from home a few days a week to avoid sixty-mile commutes. Robust, versatile information technology is in place to support telecommuting, but the management vision needed is not.

The electronic immigrants, foreign information and professional workers who provide their products via telecommunications, are firmly established sources of productivity. There are few businesses, large or small, that do not contend with international, electronic competition from labor or make use of it to the disadvantage of other companies. The global workforce is tapped for tasks large and small using telecommunications.

A publisher in a coastal resort hundreds of miles from an urban center commissions book illustrations from an artist in the Philippines—and pockets the substantial difference in charges he would otherwise have to pay an American. For a decade, Boeing Aircraft has directed the construction of commercial jetliners by engineers in Seattle, Washington, linked by telephones, computer communications, video, and inevitably, fax machines to fabricators in Japan.

Jamaica Digiport International [JDI], a joint venture of AT&T, Cable and Wireless (United Kingdom), and Telecommunications of Jamaica sells advanced telecommunications to ten data processing companies. These companies operate data-entry services in Jamaica's free trade zone; wages of the 600 employees of these firms are 10 to 20 percent of those paid in the United States for the same work.[1] A U.S. computer software company, Saztec, runs a remote data-entry facility in China where wages are two dollars a week. American Airlines has located its entire world ticketing operation in Barbados.[2] Similarly, remote data-entry and administrative operations have opened in India, Ireland, Israel, Korea, Mexico, Singapore, and Taiwan.[3] Even in the United States, prairie states are boasting of new jobs in data-entry shops reached by satellite because their prevailing wages and housing costs undercut those in the West and South.

To the dairyman in Santa Rosa, California, who manages his farm fifteen miles away by telephone, or to the aerospace company that manages the construction of fault-intolerant aircraft by telecommunications, the technology of remote work has proven itself productive, economically advantageous, and serviceable.

The professional down the hall borrows the office laptop computer to finish a project at home. The manager calls a branch well into its day's work in another time zone before leaving for his own office. The sales force meets by teleconference. Electronic mail flows in from around the world; conversations are no longer synchronous. For growing numbers of employees, telephone tag is a thing of the past. Within seven years the time spent transmitting electronic mail over "telephone" systems will exceed the time spent talking. Monthly productivity can't be measured until employees at far-flung locales upload their spreadsheets to the network hub. Many of the people we work with closely are not close at all.

The modern manager travels through computer cyberspace, wades through facsimiles, and dutifully listens to a dozen voice messages each morning. Thanks to telecommunications and computers, many workers spend far more time viewing screens than one another. At Pacific Bell, thousands of managers listen to a voice mail newsletter prepared the evening before; they retrieve it over cellular phones as they drive to work–or rather, they work as they drive.

Telephone callers to JC Penney catalog sales are routinely helped by telecommuting representatives working from their homes, physically remote from customer and company both. A group of Best Western Hotel reservation takers are inmates in a woman's prison in Arizona. Small businesses may have operations scattered around a city, because telecommunication links allow them to avoid the cost of consolidating facilities. Handshakes are still interdigital, but the digits are more frequently electronic.

Using telecommunications for remote management is not itself a new phenomenon, all of the hype of the Information Superhighway notwithstanding. Remote work, or "managing at a distance," was invented in 1857 when J. Edgar Thompson, owner of the Penn Railroad, discovered that he could use his company's private telegraph system to manage remote divisions, provided he delegated to them substantial control in their use of equipment and labor. Railroad organization followed the telegraph wire, and the outwardly mobile corporation transformed itself into a complex of decentralized operations.[4]

What *is* new is that in the private sector and the public sector, in large organizations and small, affordable, high-performance telecommunication networks have clearly become ubiquitous, vital partners in managing work. Modern organizations of every kind disperse because their own communication capabilities allow them to. With the growing physical chasms between workers within organizations and between workers and consumers filled in by information and communication systems, even the most hands-on managers quickly learn the new boundaries of the workplace. No longer is it a tidy, tangible entity. They must come to terms with remote work, managed electronically. No longer can employers rely simply on employees filing into the workplace at the appointed hour to take their appointed seats.

Management Traditions

Despite the development of global organization, remote work technologies, and telecommunication-based coordination, management practice remains tradition-bound. It relies on two forms of control: rules and visual observation of the work process. Rules tell workers what to do and observations confirm how well they do it. It's a tight, familiar formula. For the last hundred years legions of managers and supervisors, and of course their employees, have worked by it, sworn by it, and often sworn at it. The most fundamental work rules, and generally the most explicit, have stated starting-time and starting-place. The time-based organization of work was presaged in the fifteenth century when clocks were mounted in church and town hall steeples, ringing in work and worship alike. It got practical when clocks became small enough to carry around and inexpensive enough to purchase for the home.[5] The Industrial Revolution cemented place-based work. The uniform regulation of time and place of work is essential to conventional production: Labor must be physically synchronized so the output of one productive process is timed and stationed to become input to another.

Now information products (and the processes that produce them), the bulk of the GNP, are produced at one time or at one place and utilized at another time or at another place. The portion of the Western economies devoted to the storage, manipulation, retrieval, and creation of information may grow to 70 percent by the year 2000.[6]

The increasing role of remote work, distance-spanning technologies, and information-based jobs would appear to challenge the industrial tradition of "same time, same place" models of work. Synchronization is feasible among those working in different places at different times. Experience with remote work increases the alacrity with which management by observation can give way to management by objective. But will the traditional time and place rules and work accede to a more contemporary concept of management? Not necessarily.

True, the time clock is an anachronism in many organizations. But industrial models of production have been forced upon information work. Although quiet assembly lines of information workers transform pieces of information rather than physical commodities into value-laden objects, the workers go to work much as workers always have. Management by observation continues as usual even if dressed up in computing and communication systems that keep tab on work done, conversations had, and workers' perambulations to water fountains, restrooms, and snack bars. More often than not, forms of management in the Information Age differ little from those in the Industrial Age.

Changes in the technologies that bind our workplaces together require flexibility in the way we organize work. But the changes indispensable to modern management are greater still. The domestic work force is shrinking, conflicts between work and nonwork sap productivity as never before, dissatisfaction with traditional work arrangements and rewards is intense, and an intolerable commute kicks the day off.

Changing Work Force Demographics

While the global labor pool grows, ironically, the domestic supply of skilled, educated, or experienced workers dwindles. In 1970, the work force grew by nearly 3 percent a year; by 1990, its growth rate had fallen by a third to 1 percent annually. Table 1–1 summarizes the labor shortage as viewed by human resource professionals. When a surplus of workers competed for jobs, they willingly sacrificed family life to overtime and long days. Now, it is employers who compete.[7] Small businesses, especially, will be hard hit by tough competition from large employers for workers.[8]

Those willing to initiate flexible management are arguably better positioned to attract and retain employees in a tight labor market.[9] In this regard, smaller, younger organizations—including small businesses—may find establishing flexible management easier than tradition-bound firms. They may compete successfully for workers despite the higher pay and material perquisites that larger, bureaucratic firms offer favored recruits.[10]

TABLE 1-1

The Growing Labor Shortage

Readers of *Nation's Business* in a survey characterized the labor shortage:

How would you describe the supply of skilled labor for your employment needs over the next five years?

3.8%	Abundant
7.8	Above average
33.2	Adequate
55.2	Inadequate

How often are you experiencing difficulty in finding qualified workers for the jobs you must fill?

21.5%	All the time
24.8	75 percent of the time
29.6	50 percent of the time
24.2	25 percent of the time
9.7	Never

In hiring, how often do you find workers who already have the skills you need?

5.0%	All the time
14.2	75 percent of the time
29.6	50 percent of the time
43.2	25 percent of the time
8.0	Never

Source: *Nation's Business*, February, 1991.

Compounding the problem of a dwindling work force are declining educational levels. Only 5 percent of job applicants to one major employer test at seventh grade level or better. A new study claims half of all American workers are functionally illiterate.

Maintaining a stable and capable workforce claims more and more of the manager's time. In pursuit of recruits, managers will increasingly depend upon women, minorities, and the physically challenged to overcome labor shortages.[11]

Work/Family Conflicts

Family issues are certainly not new. Rather, the workforce is changing so dramatically that home and work wrestle with fresh vengeance. Women are just under half of the workforce, yet their

TABLE 1-2

Flexible Work Responses to Lifestyle Drives

Choices	Drives				
	Travel	Work	Family	Leisure	Environmental Ideology
Flextime	X		X		
Compressed work week	X		X	X	X
Telecommuting	X	X	X	X	X

Source: Adapted from Mokhtarian and Salomon, *Modeling the Choice of Telecommuting: Setting the Context.*

responsibilities for homemaking and child rearing have changed little from the days their husbands brought home the bacon and they cooked it. Today, dual income-earners characterize the American family. Single heads of households spiral in number. Elder care strains a fifth of the work force, and many are in the "sandwich generation," caring for both children and elders. The entry of large numbers of women into the workforce with no corresponding diminishment of calls on their time for household labor and family care creates a demand for scheduling flexibility.

With these social and economic changes have come new values. For both women and men, care-giving, family life, leisure, the so-called personal spheres, are typically as important as career interests. It now appears that commute avoidance and environmental ideology may also help mold some lifestyles.[12]

Many employees expect to strike balances between home and work—their ambitions have diversified. They'll often take less pay, refuse jobs, reduce hours, call in sick, strike deals with a willing manager, whatever they can do—to have it all. As Table 1–2 illustrates, lifestyle values call for flexible work arrangements. Often they quit when a compromise is unattainable.

There is an assumption that these balancers are mostly women. However, in a survey of 1,200 men in a Minneapolis firm, 70 percent of those under 35 years old report serious conflicts between work and family.[13] Many admit to turning down promotions to avoid increasing work/family conflicts. In the National debate leading to the passage of the Family and Medical Leave Act, the very low participation rate of fathers in corporate programs was often cited by both proponents (claiming the bill wouldn't hurt) and opponents (claiming the bill wouldn't help). For example, a 1988 survey of 1,000 companies found that only 1.3 percent of eligible fathers made use of family leave. But the experience of AT&T, a "family-friendly" company that has had parental leave in place since the late 1970s, tells another story. AT&T discovered that while in 1981 only one man for every 400 women took leave for a newborn, in 1992 *one man for every thirty women did so*, a jump of more than 1,300 percent.[14] If AT&T, one of the largest employers in the world, is representative, men will join women in needing more flexibility at work to accommodate their personal responsibilities.

How Workers Define Success

How are these jugglers—of either sex—to be managed? Not simply by good pay and opportunities for advancement, that much is clear.[15] Their wants have changed.[16] For example, the marginal utility of pay raises declines as a job motivator as employee compensation increases. In other words, it costs more and more, proportionally, to use money to motivate an employee whose labors are highly valued, the one companies want most to accommodate.[17] Regardless of pay level, nonfinancial rewards for work compete with and often surpass in importance financial rewards.[18]

Workers in the United States, Europe, Canada, and Japan, rate "expressive satisfaction" more important than financial satisfaction. Expressiveness is a sociologist's term for work-related motivation resulting from how interesting a job is, how much autonomy and personal achievement it permits, and whether it leads, in turn, to further opportunities for expression.[19] According to a 1993 study of 3,718 representative U.S. workers, only 21 percent said that "success in work life means making a good income."[20] Women rate opportunity to learn, convenient work hours, and a match between job requirements and their abilities as very important, while men regard a lot of autonomy as very important. For both men and women, flexible scheduling (flextime) or flexible location (telecommuting or other forms of remote work) can increase job satisfaction and facilitate both employee recruiting and retention.[21]

Commuting

Like taxes and weather, the commute seems beyond control. Traffic jams star in movies such as *Speed* because audiences groan with identification. The United State is unique in the world not only for its unquenchable love of the automobile, but for its nearly universal neglect of any transportation alternative. The result is an increasingly inefficient commitment of the day both to traveling and driving. Companies historically encourage commuting by car by providing free parking, a capital cost subsidized by tax deductions; they are not "felt" expenditures by either the company or the workforce.[22] Governments do the same by limiting the convenience of mass transit and by financing freeway construction. Housing shortages, caused by price or occupancy, encourage longer commutes.

Mass commuting (the opposite of mass transit) is a ticking time bomb. Traffic delays caused by inadequate roads are expected to cost the United States $50 billion by the year 2005 in wasted wages and gasoline.[23] In California, traffic congestion is estimated to cost employers $2.4 million *a day* in productivity losses.[24] More than 60 percent of paved highways in the United States need rehabilitation, and more than 40 percent of bridges longer than 20 feet are structurally deficient or functionally obsolete. Yet from 1980 to 1990 the number of highway miles travelled annually increased by a third, to 3 trillion.[25] Air pollution, health losses from both accident and disease, wastes of time, employee frustration, and stress are toxic byproducts of mass commuting that are becoming as unacceptable as secondary smoke from a cigarette.

There is no question that commuting increases stress and creates a negative attitude that workers, particularly women, bring into the home.[26] Job-related stress, in turn, has recently been linked to a fivefold increased risk of colorectal cancer.[27]

A malady in its own right, stress is now the leading cause of job disability claims. In California, for example, the number of job stress claims jumped from 1,178 in 1979 to 9,368 in 1988, the most recent period studied; correcting for growth in the workforce, that is an increase of 540 percent. "Job pressures" were cited 69 percent of the time. Fifty-five percent of the claims were from women, and women filing stress-related claims were double the numbers of those of women filing for *all other reasons*. A spokesperson for the California Casualty Group, one of the state's major disability underwriters, blames "work and family balancing" for the increase.[28] However, stress (especially for women) is also generated by commuting.[29]

The search for jobs will make commuting worse. Seventy-five percent of new jobs are in the suburbs, but 57 percent of African-Americans and 49 percent of Hispanics live in inner cities. These minority populations as well as suburbanites must travel to work by car; commuting between suburbs or from cities to suburbs is nearly impossible by other means.[30,31]

Environmental measures coupled with a crisis-prone transportation system and miserable commutes are forcing institutions to confront their contributions to traffic congestion, vehicular air pollution, fuel consumption, and wear and tear on the transportation infrastructure. With the passage of the National Clean Air Act, there is a broad statutory mandate for employers to reduce the congestion caused by single-occupied vehicles.

Since 1983, when a professor of civil engineering suggested reducing the demand for transportation rather than trying to increase its supply, flexible work has been advocated, studied, and more recently, supported by regulation to moderate the commuter crisis.[32] The feasibility of his proposal lodges more than he ever imagined in the capacity of telecommunications to short-circuit distance.

The Frontiers of Time and Space

Time and space are the frontiers of modern organization. To a globalist, these frontiers are as obvious as different time zones, varying holidays, inconsistent work hours, distant markets, and shipping rates. Indeed, the 168-hour work week flourishes as the "movement of the sun and the economy both never stop in the global economy."[33] Airline and hotel reservation systems, telemarketing operations, transnational electronic fund transfers, satellite communication and control systems, tens of thousands of computer, communication, and electrical networks, robot-run factories that work oblivious to the earth's rotation, globally dispersed government agencies, broadcast services, and even supermarkets run day and night, seven days a week, 365 days a year, around the world.[34]

To a localist, these frontiers are becoming as obvious as a worker absent while caring for a sick parent, a valuable programmer away from work on maternity leave, an irritable commuter filing for disability caused by stress, a jammed office without room for one more employee, or an office computer system so choked that it doesn't really work right until nearly everyone has left for the day. These are the burdens of time and space borne by organizations and their employees–until they decide to do something about it.

In this century, Albert Einstein mended scientific concepts of time and space. He showed that they are not rigid, precise coordinates mapping every action, but are fluid, flexible, and relative. Concepts of industrial time and space are undergoing similar transformations. Monolithic time, the workday, bounded by a monolithic space, the workplace, are not the absolutes that morning rush hour and rectangular office buildings imply. The centralization of the industrial revolution is giving way to the decentralization of the information revolution.

As a result of this shift in thinking, managers restructure the hours and locations of jobs as covariables to optimize, and in allowing their sharp delineations to yield, take advantage of their interdependence. Permit the selection of more convenient, less distant work places, and workers' uses of time markedly improve. Change a work schedule, and the physical corridors of commuting and communications become more efficient. Over the past twenty years, management flexibility has reliably increased productivity by reducing conflicts between home and work, by reducing commutes, and by a congruent increase in use of telecommunications and computing.

Today, these enumerations are almost prosaic. In only two decades, the future has caught up with the futurists. Over this slight span of years, management has slowly, very slowly, evolved. At first, flexible work was a grassroots movement, a private arrangement struck between managers and individual employees who wanted to work from home, adjust reporting times, or otherwise flex their jobs. More and more companies experimented with flextime, then telecommuting. Today, employers are recognizing that they stand to benefit from flexibility as much as their employees. Now they must formalize into durable policies and programs years of ad hoc activity.[35]

This book offers human resource departments, public and private sector managers, supervisors, and employees a guide to telecommuting, flextime, and remote work centers as practical, cost-effective solutions to today's challenges.

2

What Is Flexible Work?

S ome managers worry that flexible work will be a radical reorga-
nization of their workplaces. However, any large organization is
likely to have people working at different shifts and at different
sites. As well, supervisors sometimes offer individual employees lat-
itude on their schedule or workplace, especially for limited periods.

One way to define telecommuting is by analogy to quite familiar
work arrangements. Among managerial and professional workers,
unofficial telecommuting is widespread—as uncelebrated, uncompensated overtime work at home. In a survey of readers of *Modern
Office Technology* magazine, 95 percent sometimes worked overtime at home and 39 percent did so every week. Here's one breakdown of just how many professionals and managers do so each
week:[1]

- 24.9 percent of systems and information managers
- 30.1 percent of administrative or operating managers
- 72.4 percent of corporate executives

Among these classes of workers, in fact, overtime telecommuting
is so common it is rarely recognized for what it is. Some 40 percent
of all home computers are purchased for this purpose. Overtime
workers—they are also called supplementers—are remote workers;
they're just working on their own time in their own space without
official sanction.

Telecommuting, with its invocation of telecommunications,

15

seems novel. On the contrary, many telecommuting professionals are simply working the regular, scheduled workday in the same way they do in the evening or on weekends. The supplementers become substitutors. Flexible schedules and work sites become formal, managed variables in the ways workers perform work.

Overtime illustrates the rewards of telecommuting. People take work home after hours for reasons very similar to those which motivate telecommuting:[2]

- Avoiding interruptions by working at home (69.4 percent)
- Meeting deadlines (54 percent)
- Making up for insufficient office time (52.9 percent)
- Making additional telephone calls (25 percent)
- Scheduling off-site, after-hour meetings (20.7 percent)
- Having better working conditions (18.8 percent)
- Compensating for staff shortages (15.6 percent)

In a survey of data processing professionals, the main reasons for working at home included improved productivity and an opportunity for some family interaction. "They could share regular meal time with their families and be physically present in the evening hours, even though toiling over their terminals."[3]

The types of professional work performed at home include:

- Reading (69.7 percent)
- Strategy and planning (51.4 percent)
- Correspondence and dictation (37.1 percent)
- Research (35.6 percent)
- Preparing speeches and presentations (34.3 percent)
- Confidential (29.7 percent)
- Financial planning (27.1 percent)
- Record keeping (22.1 percent)
- Sales (7.1 percent).

Although overtime work at home is rarely instigated by an official program, it frequently receives organizational assistance from employers and designated space by employees. Of the supplementers surveyed above, some 39 percent set up specific areas in their homes for remote work and an astonishing 77 percent received funds from their employers for home computing equipment. However, only 20 percent received additional compensation for home labors. Of those who did, many receive soft compensation such as extra vacation time, longer lunch hours, extra time off, or a company car.[4]

These figures demonstrate that for many managerial and professional workers, their personal adoption of telecommuting would require little more than a shift in perspective—an acknowledgement that the reasons why people work overtime at home can become a rationale for working at home during regular shifts.

However, for a manager to authorize telecommuting for other employees requires a considerably greater change in thinking. Overtime worked at home is gratis, a fulfillment of an unwritten rule that says professional and managerial salary scales and status compensate the fifty-two-hour work week. Since this overtime is an invisible contribution, its regular location (home) and hours (weekends, evenings) are ignored. To support flexibility the manager must stop viewing work at home as merely supplemental and see it instead as a technique to improve productivity.

Unfortunately, the phrase *flexible work* is used to describe a wide variety of work arrangements which have little similarity to one another. Unless concepts are clear, they cannot reliably answer anything. Variations among flexible work programs have been slighted, profoundly distorting their impacts, benefits, and problems.[5] For instance, many potential disadvantages of telecommuting arise only when people work full-time at home. Concerns about a telecommuter's lack of visibility in an office, or about the availability of staff for unexpected assignments are resolved by telecommuting only for part of the work week.[6] Hence, the federal government, in initiating a flexible work program, takes special care to contrast its telecommuting program from other forms of home-based work:

> [When] Federal employees to work at home or at other approved sites away from the office for all or part of the work week . . ., such alternative work arrangements are known as flexible workplace arrangements . . . *[They] should not be confused with home-based business . . . or independent contractor arrangements in the home.* [emphasis added][7]

Flexible management described in this book comes in three flavors: flextime, flexiplace (remote work), and telecommuting. To avoid the definitional mayhem common in popular writings, we must agree on our use of these terms.

Flextime

The oldest and most widely adopted form of flexible work is *flextime*. Because flextime policies prepare organizations for the greater complexities of managing telecommuting and remote work centers, it logically comes first. Flextime, as used in this book, always refers to full-time employment at hours that vary from the standard weekly schedule. Starting time, ending time, and lunch hour all can change.

Some companies include arrangements such as job-sharing, part-time employment, contract work, and peak-time work (on-call work arrangements) in flexibility scheduling. The recommendations in this book, however, deal with alternative ways to manage *full-time* employees, the bedrock of all organizations.

Some companies have offered flextime options to their workers for decades. McClellan Air Force base in California, for example, has allowed its 13,000 employees to vary daily starting and ending times since 1969.[8] Some researchers conclude that 93 percent of American companies permit flexible scheduling for some employees, but in practice no more than 30 percent of employees may actually have flextime alternatives.[9,10,11] Flextime is readily diagrammed in the figure shown.

Core time is time that flextime employees must be on the job. The variable stretches of starting times and quitting times are *bandwidths*. A flextime schedule, then, fits into the work day based on bandwidth, core time, particular requirements of the job, organizational policies, and individual objectives.

A company may fix choices of starting time or create long core hours that leave little room for maneuvering schedules, a limitation of flextime that may lessen its usefulness to some employees. For example, school closures and other unpredictable family responsibilities may create a sudden need for flexibility in starting time unique to that day.

Contemporary versions of flextime increasingly add allowance for midday absences from work; employees can reschedule and extend lunch hours, and repay time away later in the same day or within a specified number of days. Employees can then keep appointments with pediatricians for sick children, for example, without calling in sick themselves.

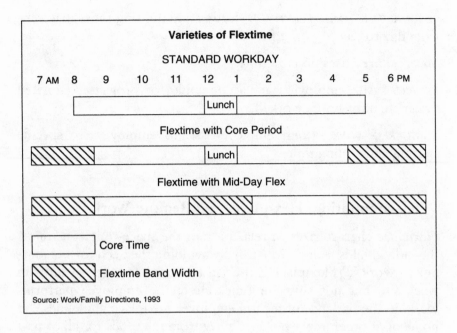

Forms of flextime include:

BANKED TIME: allows workers to bank hours that they may then apply as compensatory time off

COMPRESSED WORK WEEK: employees complete forty or eighty working hours in fewer than five or ten days

CORE TIME: employees must be at-work during specified hours each day of scheduled work

E-TIME: employees may take excused time off, without pay, whenever work load permits

FIXED FLEXTIME PROGRAMS: employees choose from among fixed, alternative work schedules

FLEXITOUR: fixed starting and quitting times are chosen by employees for a work period, but may vary from period to period

FULL FLEXTIME: employees make independent decisions about a combination of scheduled hours that total forty or eighty hours over a week or two-week period

GLIDING TIME (DAILY FLEXTIME): starting and quitting times may vary from day to day

MAXIFLEX: requires no core time

PROJECT TIME: employees are accountable for projects completed rather than for hours worked

STAGGERED WORK HOURS: employer assigns employees to specific starting and ending times.[12]

Telecommuting, Flexiplace, and Remote Work Centers

Flexiplace characterizes "a relaxation of the space-time constraints the individual is facing, primarily by avoiding the need for the journey to work."[13] Flexiplace is used in this book to refer to shifts in work site but not shifts in time. Here, the employee performs work, in the parlance of federal employee flexiplace guidelines, "at home or at other approved sites away from the office for all or part of the work week." Again, in this book, flexiplace refers exclusively to work arrangements of full-time employees.

Flexiplace echoes remote work arrangements that are quite recognizable. For example, it resembles the remote work arrangements of electronic immigrants and workers dispersed among decentralized units of a company.[14] Home-based telecommuting (when work hours are specified as a shift), remote work centers, neighborhood work centers, satellite work centers, telework centers, telecottages, and even mobile work centers are all types of flexiplace programs.

When an employee combines flexiplace, flextime, and electronic communication, the result is *telecommuting*. The common elements of flextime, flexiplace, and telecommuting are illustrated in the figure shown. Telecommuting originally only referred to transferring work from the office to the home using telecommunications.[15] Now, the telecommuters include those who labor at remote work centers or at home.

Although telecommuting does not incorporate flextime in some usages (and so becomes identical to flexiplace), there are semantic, programmatic, and productivity arguments to link the two. Telecommuters rarely observe regular office schedules because they

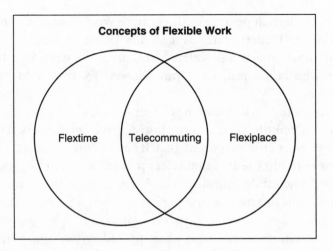

Concepts of Flexible Work

Flextime   Telecommuting   Flexiplace

can easily shift their working hours and because, as a rule, they are more productive when they do make such shifts. In one study, more than 90 percent of all telecommuters flexed their time, starting earlier, taking some time off, and working in the evening; most reported improvements in productivity as a result.[16]

Therefore, flextime is compatible with telecommuting but distinct from it. Flexiplace arrangements may or may not incorporate flextime; conversely, flextime may or may not incorporate flexiplace arrangements. Thus, people who work at remote work centers are usually granted twenty-four-hour access to their offices and often clock irregular clusters of hours when policy allows. Flexible work may include both. For some organizations, only flextime or only flexiplace arrangements may be most appropriate; in others, flexing both time and place of work will be more beneficial; in most organizations, flexible management will experiment with all forms of alternative work arrangements and the best mix—usually involving all three—develops over time.

Remote Work Centers

Transportation designers in the United States, land use planners in Europe, and developers and technologists in Japan are heralding the latest institutionalization of flexible work, the remote work center. They consider it the ultimate successor to home-based telecommuting and even the model of the work place of the future.[17]

In its modern appearance, the remote work center was first conceived in the United States as a facility that provides conveniently located office space and related resources to would-be telecommuters who could not, were not allowed to, or would not work from home.

The remote work center has several forms. The *satellite center* describes a remote work center housing telecommuters from only one employer; it is proposed that from twenty to more than 100 employees might use it. Satellite centers are a new application of an old trend toward decentralization. *Local centers*, in contrast, house workers from different employers who form a partnership to construct and maintain remote work facilities. *Neighborhood centers* are micro remote work centers that provide space and resources to employees (from the same or different employers) commuting to it from within a small, contiguous area.[18]

Local centers have had trouble overcoming security concerns. Companies asked to join a cooperative remote work center worry most about their secrets being compromised. In Sweden, remote work centers countered with ground rules prohibiting two companies in the same line of business (say, two banks) from participating at the same time in the same center.[19] They believed that the close proximity of employees would naturally lead to revealing chit-chats or rummaging of computer files.

A number of U.S. projects have suffered because of security concerns by participants or invitees, especially where open space (offices without walls) was used to reduce interior construction costs. Even worse, shared technological environments, for example a computer network provided by the center, greatly heightened security concerns. Perhaps for this reason, single-company projects appear to be faring better than those based on multiple tenancy.

Intriguing remote work centers (most of which are outside of the United States, unfortunately), have now been set up at great distances from an employer to tap a workforce that would otherwise be unavailable, to generate new jobs where they are needed, or to take advantage of better priced land, labor, or employee housing. Frequently these facilities are purposely located in job-starved rural areas, but not always. In other countries, these distant facilities are called telecottages. The word recalls Alvin Toffler's coinage, "electronic cottage" in his prediction of telecommuting in *The Third Wave*.

In Sweden, the world's first telecottage was founded in the early 1980s by the federal government as a way to move jobs from the national capital to outlying areas with high unemployment.[20] Now, telecottages are also planned or in operation in Norway, Japan, Great Britain (Scotland, England, and Ireland), Australia, Benin, India, Indonesia, Nigeria, Papua New Guinea, Sri Lanka, the United Republic of Tanzania, and several Latin American countries.[21] In Ireland, a telecottage combines electronic immigration with remote work in a rural areas with high unemployment; people there perform data entry for an American firm.[22] A British manufacturer, Fokker Aircraft Industries, has built a telecottage employing twenty-two workers in a rural area.[33] Australia organized a world convocation on telecottages in 1993 and has one successful telecottage project well underway.[24]

In the United States, telecottages have been developed by a number of firms. The Norrell Company, a temporary employment agency, opened telecottages in Atlanta, Georgia, and Memphis, Tennessee, successfully recruiting data-entry clerks.[25] Companies, individually and in concert are opening high-tech billing, fulfillment, and credit card processing centers in the Midwest where land and housing are affordable, the workforce eager and available, and wages on average lower. Data is shipped to these centers electronically. These are not cottages, of course, in the physical sense; they are medium- to large-size company operations.

One U.S. company based in Los Angeles moved clerical workers who before had commuted to headquarters located in the central business district into a satellite operation. Staffing requirements were decreased by 15 percent because of improved productivity. Turnover dropped from 73 to 45 percent, saving an estimated $600 per employee or $350,000 annually in costs such as training. The company gave downtown workers a $10-a-week bonus because the commute into the city is so onerous that recruitment is difficult; the incentive was unnecessary at the satellite center. For employees, merely reducing commuting by at least eleven miles a day compensated in out-of-pocket savings for the loss of the incentive.[26]

Pacific Bell operates satellite work centers in San Francisco, to avoid a congested commute to headquarters located across the San Francisco Bay in San Ramon, California, and in an outlying area of

Los Angeles. The Los Angeles center, used by professionals who want to reduce their commuting time, has an absenteeism rate 25 percent less than the company average.[27]

In other locales, technologies have combined to encourage workplace decentralization. Two Xerox Corporation work groups, one in Palo Alto, California, the other in Portland, Oregon, used audio, video, and computer linkages to test communications between so-called super workstations, minicomputers in a personal computer box. In Ontario, Canada, various ministries and the Worker's Compensation Board relocated some offices to smaller towns to distribute government jobs and reduce commuting, linking them back to headquarters' data networks.[28] Private companies in Ontario have followed suit searching for lower rents and easier commutes.[29]

The Ontario Comm Center, located in a gridlocked county near Los Angeles, California, is an ambitious effort to retail the remote work center. The center is owned and operated by a private company; tenants purchase various packages of office space, telecommunications, and computer systems. What makes the center different from executive suites are its secretarial and reception personnel trained to personalize their services for each tenant; they camouflage what is essentially an impersonal answering service.[30] The center, from a tenant's perspective, is an instant remote work center: just add employees and furniture. Pricing of the Comm Center is competitive with good quality office space in the region.

An interesting comparison of the effects of different forms of remote work on the utilization of space and time is provided by David Gann's study of Japenese remote work centers, as in the figure shown.

For some years, building developers have been experimenting with shared tenant services, particularly shared telecommunications facilities such as switches (PBXs), built-in, plug-ready wiring infrastructure, security systems, computer-controlled heating and air conditioning, and other popular technological facilities. These so-called smart buildings have had a mixed reception; they are getting boosted, however, by the remote work center concept. Remote work centers rely heavily on telecommunications to maintain organizational contact with headquarters, to ship work products created

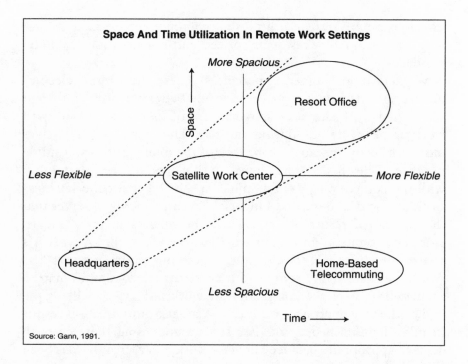

Space And Time Utilization In Remote Work Settings

Source: Gann, 1991.

on computers, and to provide access to corporate information located on distant mainframe computers. In a related vein, a number of housing developments in northern California are gearing up for telecommuters. Advanced telecommunications services, wiring infrastructure, and a room specifically designed to become a home office are built into each house.

Not Just Offices, Anymore

Japanese corporations are developing so-called resort offices. Sited in well-regarded vacation areas, they house professionals, sometimes with their families, always with their work groups, for two to four weeks. There, their schedules mix work and recreation; often, a group will be assigned a project to complete. The hotellike facilities incorporate communications and computing resources, various sleeping room/office configurations, and access to the amenities of the area. The resort office provides an escape from work-related stress. The concept reverberates in the United States in the occasional corporate retreat at a plush conference center. Japanese resort office stays are reasonably priced and not luxurious by hotel standards.[31]

Workers report mixed experiences. These short-term telecommuters felt themselves more creative and better able to plan than at their usual work site because of control of time and the ability to work at peak periods during the day. They believed themselves more productive because of the lack of the interruptions so routine in offices. They had a "rare chance to think about their relationship with the company."[32] Wendy Spinks, a researcher for the Japanese Institute for Economic and Financial Research, wryly observes that the success of resort offices reflects the failures of the standard work environment, an insight worth some reflection.[33] A worker's control of work time, for example, should not require a resort.

On the other hand, some had their resort telecommutes marred by insecurity over the completion of work tasks, especially as the end of the stay approaches and an initial lack of motivation results in pile of unfinished work. For some, supervising themselves to achieve appropriate balance between work and recreation has been difficult.[34]

The very newest remote work structure is not a distant building, but desk space that is not assigned to any single individual; instead, it is allocated (sometimes by reservation) to whomever wants it for a short period. The concept is popular in organizations where employees regularly travel to distant divisions to do their work and where sales forces don't need an assigned office.

Various implementations include hoteling, nonterritorial office, or in Canada, the floating office. These are systems of temporarily assigned workspace.[35] In one particularly ambitious program, the international consulting firm Ernst and Young has a hoteling coordinator, a policy of providing a desk environment equivalent to that enjoyed by a nonmobile employee with the same organizational status, and lockers for personal papers, work in progress, and desk items. Ernst and Young predicts it will eventually be able to eliminate 2 million square feet of rental office space (out of 7 million) for an annual savings of some $40 million through hoteling because the ratio of hoteling employees to desk space is five to one.[36]

Hewlett-Packard has extended the concept to computer workstations that are temporarily assigned. IBM has "free addresses", namely offices that can be used by anyone without reservation. The first coinage of these concepts, apparently, was in the Navy; called hotdesking by sailors, it pejoratively refers to bunks used by different sailors on different watches (the bunk being warmed by the previous occupant). That term was revised by Hewlett-Packard to Red Carpet to give it a more appropriate, corporate connotation![37]

Advantages Over Home-Based Telecommuting

Remote work centers have several advantages over home-based telecommuting. By bringing together employees under a common roof, it is possible to enjoy economies of scale in space, equipment, telecommunications, reception, and other traditional work resources which are often uneconomic for home-based telecommuting.[38] Local work centers can also increase economies of scale by pooling the facility budgets of different organizations.

Although the problem of loneliness among home-based telecommuters appears to be exaggerated, for those telecommuters who miss office social life, the remote work center could be a good compromise.[39] On the other side, some telecommuters may find working at home too distracting and relish somewhat conventional office society without the hassles of commuting to and parking in congested areas.

The remote work center may effectively combine the management techniques of a traditional workplace with the commute-reduction benefits of telecommuting. For example, a remote work center can include supervisors drawn from a participating department or even from another department.[40]

Many employees who would like to telecommute lack an adequate home environment in which to do so. Remote work centers are of interest in Hawaii because high housing costs mean employees move into small residential structures with too little space in which to set up a home office.[41] Furthermore, if the number of telecommuters in an area grows, it may be efficient to transfer them from home-based telecommuting to a remote work center.

Unlike home/offices, remote work centers are not financed in any way by the telecommuters who use them. Workers function as they might if they were not telecommuting, with only modest distinctions. As a result, one telecommuting advisory group suggests that centers need not be staffed only by workers who volunteer to telecommute, in contrast to home-based telecommuting which is almost always voluntary.[42]

Developing Remote Work Centers

Although the remote work center incurs facility costs, it can be financially attractive when a organization needs new space. Distant properties may usually be acquired at more favorable prices because they do not suffer the speculation or high overhead that often afflict suburban or urban parcels favored as sites of corporate headquarters.

The possibility of positive economic impact—not only in salaries, but in improved tax-bases—leads some communities to encourage remote work center development and to incorporate centers, for example, in general plans. Their inducements to employers may eventually take the form of tax forgiveness, commodious zoning, deals with telecommunication providers to upgrade facilities, and other sweeteners long used by communities to support job creation. In Japan and Sweden, the remote work center is now a cornerstone of government land, economic, and technological development programs.[43] Exurban communities in California, beyond the suburbs, are experimenting with these inducements. Remote work centers can mean financial gain for the employer, for the center's landlord, for employees with reduced commuting, and for the community that hosts the project.

The Japanese are using the allure of remote centers to attract professional jobs and professionals. One enterprising community far from any large city established a "U-turn" project, an office that provides free employment search services in Tokyo to encourage former residents to return, that is, to make a "U-turn" in their working *and* personal lives. Several hundred professionals have been placed in jobs in the community where they grew up but left after graduating from college. An "I-turn" program encourages professionals unhappy with city life to "emmigrate" into a rural area. In both instances, the telecottage has been the anchor of attractive, professional jobs.

The Southern California Association of Governments was able

to establish a more responsive image with its clients (city governments) in an area by setting up a small remote work center in a city hall distant from its headquarters.[44] The League of California Cities has tried to extend this application of remote work in a program it calls the mobile city government. The objective is to "separate the production of services from their delivery . . ."[45] by moving work closer to the worker residences and services closer to their consumers. Thus, for example, a building permit agency might have small branch offices dispersed throughout a city so that neither applicants or staff would have to travel downtown.

U.S. professionals, in effect, are attempting I-turns themselves. "They want it all: the stimulation of a first class job with the ambience of a simpler life style."[46] Professionals are selecting life in "penturbia," a term proposed by David Heenan to characterize outlying towns of 200,000 or fewer people at least fifty miles from a major city, which benefit from close association with "universities, state capitals, research parks or other institutions" imparting "diversity and cultural spark."[47] An impressive list of medium and large companies have relocated their headquarters to just such penturban areas.

Fortune magazine also detects a breed of professionals—"yiffies" (young, individualistic, freedom-minded, and few)—who

> insist on getting satisfaction from their jobs, but they refuse to make personal sacrifices for the sake of the corporation. . . . Yiffies are confident that their skills and educational credentials will carry them through life. This knowledge-is-power mentality makes them feel untied, free to pursue unpredictable paths.[48]

How to manage the yiffies? Since job satisfaction is so important to them, according to *Fortune*, offer them freedom and flexibility.[49] Whether Yiffies are replacing Yuppies is hard to say, but changing values are more than evident in the workforce. As this trend grows, it will begin to motivate an American telecottage movement.

Work centers can have several different objectives that make their costs more justifiable. For example, they might function as bus terminals for charters taking employees to a company's headquarters. In many areas, buses have special lanes on freeways and bridges to encourage their use—making them attractive alternatives to the car commute—whereas land for parking may be much cheaper in outlying areas. A number of junior colleges have in effect set up remote work centers for their faculty and remote classroom locations for students. One junior college in California ships instruction to a remote facility via closed-circuit television, effectively doubling the number of students who can take a course and expanding the service area. A Swedish work environment specialist proposes that a remote work center might set up a for-profit child care center which need not limit its clients to employees, and thus become more feasible economically.[50]

Both advanced industrial societies and developing countries are accumulating practical experience with remote work by publicly financing center start-ups. In Japan, private sector consortia including banks, construction companies, developers, telecommunication, and computer companies have led in establishing remote work centers. The Japanese have been particularly motivated by the soaring cost of office space in urban areas, especially in Tokyo, and the overcrowding of offices and transit systems with resulting drops in productivity. Home-based telecommuting has proved impractical, however, on a large scale. Houses are typically too small to accommodate a home office, and Japanese businesses increasingly count on sophisticated telecommunication services that are rare in residences.[51,52]

The level of experimentation in flexibility has been sufficient to create a new profession, the building engineer. These experts help construction companies incorporate advanced information technologies in buildings far from the rich telecommunication infrastructure of the Japanese city. The results have generally been quite positive.[53]

In the United States, the federal government and a number of states have experimented with remote work centers by subsidizing center rents, underwriting scholarly research into their operations, and encouraging private support through partnerships.

For example, California has made funds available, contingent upon matching monies from counties and private companies, for the construction, operation, and observation of remote work centers. Kentucky has designed and partially funded a telecottage to stimulate rural job development. Hawaii launched a satellite facility with impressive private sector support (especially equipment donations). The state of Washington organized a remote work center in a Seattle suburb.

The state-financed center in Washington was very successful until subsidies ran out. Both government agencies and private companies were unwilling to pay market level rents for telecommuting facilities, and the center depended on below-market rents made possible by state sponsorship. The Washington State center folded after the subsidies were eliminated in state budget cutbacks.

Who Works at Remote Work Centers

Are remote work centers primarily designed for professionals? There are two significant barriers to the flexible management of a large numbers of workers and especially of nonprofessional workers: resistance to managing by objective, and differing views among managers of the autonomy or self-direction of professional compared to classified or nonexempt workers. The first, management by objective (MBO), is essential whenever a worker is out of the line of sight. The second, autonomy, authorizes the degree of independence and self-reliance a worker is allowed.

Autonomy is granted by remote work. A telecommuter in a Swedish local work center (housing different companies) declared, "No one was actually dependent precisely on me nor I on anyone else . . . There was no need to show off. . . ." Instead, the professionals cooperated with one another on technical matters such as computer operations.[54] Professionals found themselves relying on themselves in new ways, from typing up a report to tinkering with software. Comparable autonomy, however, is rarely granted clerical and other nonexempt workers.

Although there are quite a few remote work centers housing classified jobs such as data-entry clerking, there is lively debate over whether centers with classified workers can succeed. Several European centers closed when remote classified workers were laid off in a recession, while those working at the headquarters directly supporting professionals were not—they were perceived as more valuable. Organizations using these centers made a priority of professional positions at headquarters.[55] A clear division of value was applied to rural, isolated, and less skilled workers.

The Future of Remote Work Centers

Remote work centers of various kinds will continue to start up. Companies and government agencies that favor decentralization may combine its familiar advantages with the commuter, lifestyle, recruitment, and retention objectives that the remote work center incorporates. Governments will continue and probably expand subsidized experiments; interested organizations may well be on the lookout for government-primed opportunities.

Because of the complex and somewhat costly facility investments required by remote work centers, there cannot be a generic prescription for how they should be implemented. Each one has to be built by hand, so to speak.

In Europe, Asia, Australia, and the Caribbean, among other locations, remote work centers will increasingly serve both domestic and international organizations. They will clearly benefit from enthusiastic federal, offshore, and private sector investments of progressive intensity.

It is premature to settle exactly how remote work centers benefit, mistreat, or otherwise impact organizations, families, communities, and employees. Consequently, the following discussions underscore flextime and home-based telecommuting as possible options. Nonetheless, economic impact from remote work centers is certain in many work places, in many countries.

Does Technology Define Flexible Work?

The "tele" in telecommuting and telecottages evokes telecommunications, the substitution of electronic communication for natural speech, images, and paper-bound information. Some but by no means all telecommuters do rely on sophisticated computer systems, facsimile machines, and other equipment less commonly found outside of offices. While telecommuting can elaborately apply information technology, it can be also be "accomplished with no more exotic a technology than a telephone."[56]

Pacific Bell, a local telephone company in California and an aggressive proponent of telecommuting, says telecommuters work by "substituting telecommunications for work-related travel"[57] and equips some of its telecommuters with little more than a telephone and others with an array of equipment including computers, facsimile machines, pagers, and multi–line telephone systems. These tools are supported by equally elaborate information structures— voice mail, electronic mail, remote database access, custom software, and telecommunication networks—far more versatile than those in most homes today. As Chapter 7 explores, although technology plays an important role in many flexible work arrangements, there is no technological imperative, no list of "must have" gadgets. Flexible work is not primarily a technological concept, it is a management concept.

Conclusion

Flexible work, despite its reputation, is not so unfamiliar; to millions of workers and thousands of managers flextime, overtime, travel, and work at remote facilities provides a relevant preview. There is no reason to anticipate flexible work as something unusual or menacing.

Among full-time employees, flexible work takes the form of flextime, telecommuting, and remote work—and various combinations of them. Flexible work arrangements are shifts in hours and work locations; although most telecommuting is still home-based, remote work centers attract worldwide interest and experimentation. In many countries, remote work centers are emerging as a component of economic development strategies. In the United States and Canada the floating office turns ordinary desk space into a remote work center.

3

Flexible Work for a Diverse Work Force

M anaging how people come to work, do their work, and leave work was defined by 1870, perfected by 1930, and has changed little since. Juxtaposed to this tradition is a workforce fundamentally different than it was even two decades ago, much less a hundred years ago. Women (most of whom are or will become mothers), ethnic minorities, the foreign-born, and older employees are the new majority. Workers who care for spouses, children, elders, lovers, and friends are almost a majority. Workforce growth has slowed dramatically. Yet a highly diversified workforce continues to be managed as if it were a homogeneous, plentiful resource ready to meet employer needs largely on employer terms.

New Management Strategies are Needed

Does a changing workforce oblige a new management strategy? The evidence is overwhelming. The organizational costs of clinging to management traditions are going up. Today's workforce requires specific management strategies to maintain productivity and stability. A closer look tells why.

Labor Shortages

The era of an abundant supply of young, white, native, male workers has ended. The workforce is neither so young, so white, nor so male—and it is not abundant. In the last ten years, growth of the workforce declined from 2.9 percent annually to 1 percent annually.[1]

Organizations compete fiercely for trained, skilled, and educated recruits. With their comparatively modest salary scales and benefits packages small businesses will have an especially hard fight for these coveted hires. Large firms will have a tough time recruiting if they try to expand operations solely with young, skilled workers; many will relocate in foreign countries because they won't be able to hire enough widget makers in America.

In competing to hire and keep the best workers, U.S. companies will find flexibility an attractive lure. In a survey of companies that use or plan to use flexible work arrangements, 62 percent cited retention as their reason, and another 14 percent cited changed workforce demographics, a congruent issue.[2] Flexibility improved recruitment according to 39 percent of the respondents, 9 percent used telecommuting as an inducement in recruiting, and 19 percent said they would eventually start using flexibility to bolster recruitment.[3] Many organizations are finding that flexible work is not just a perk that attracts good workers, but a necessary accommodation.

The Disabled Worker

The 43 million Americans with disabilities are about 18 percent of the population. Of those disabled individuals who could work, an astonishing 85 percent are not employed.[4] However, with the passage of the Americans With Disabilities Act (ADA), employers who disregard the working interests of the disabled not only deny themselves a broader pool of workers from which to draw, but expose their companies to serious antidiscrimination litigation.

To what extent can flexible work engage contributions of disabled workers? Some disabled workers must either work from home or may not be able to work at all.[5,6] Programs run by a number of computer-intensive employers, including the American Express Corporation in New York and the Dataserv Corporation in Minnesota, show that a telecommuting program can enable long-term employment of the disabled. In these demonstration projects, severely disabled individuals with appropriate, adaptive computer technology in the home became productive, career employees.

On the other hand, telecommuting could be used by an employer to avoid the challenges of mainstreaming, that is, striving to assure that disabled individuals participate in organizational life. Disabled employees must never be segregated from the workforce by pushing them into telecommuter roles. As with nearly all other telecommuters, their work-at-home arrangements must be voluntary.

If a position can be filled by a telecommuter and a disabled employee wishes to telecommute, the employer has to agree to how equipment, communication, and information resource costs will be allocated between them. Many institutions and community services offer financial, technical, or equipment support to assist disabled people to work in the office or the home.

Note that for some employees with disabilities, flextime will be of assistance because it allows the workday to be broken up into segments of work and rest. Some employees with disabilities will need to rest because of the exertion of commuting or of work.[7] The similarity between using flexible work to retain the services of the temporarily disabled (for example, those on maternity leave) and the permanently disabled (for example, those with chronic illnesses such as AIDS) is instructive.

The Working Family

In the workforce as a whole, the most important propellant of flexible work is the change in our family and household structures. No longer do we have fathers and husbands at work, and mothers and wives at home taking care of the children and house. Only one family in twelve combines a "bread winner with a bread baker."[8] In fact, there is a slightly greater percentage of single, female heads of households in the workplace than there are of husbands belonging to traditional families.[9]

Already, at least 40 percent of the workforce belongs to dual income families and another 6 to 8 percent are single heads of households.[10] Together, these modern households with children are nearly half of the workforce. All but 12 percent of the remainder of the workforce are single, from households without children, or from so-called nontraditional, significant other relationships.

Economic necessity drives this change. In 1973, households financed by a man over thirty earned on average $25,253 per year (in 1988 dollars). By 1988, in same year dollars, the income was valued at $18,763, a loss of 25 percent. Forty percent of married women in 1988 had partners earning less than $15,000 a year.[11] Thus, to live *only as well* as a family did twenty years ago almost always requires two—sometimes three—incomes. The notion that women work for pin money to fatten discretionary income is without basis; women, like men, need to work.

Since nearly 90 percent of working women become mothers at some point in their work life, the meteoric rise of women in the workplace deserves special note.[12] By the year 2000, women will start a first job twice as often as men do, and become 47 percent of the work force, an increase of 20 percent in only eleven years. Presently, women are 44 percent of the work force and occupy a third of middle- and upper-management positions.[13,14] Over the last ten years, the number of women professionals and managers has increased two-and-a-half times, and in certain professions—law, medicine, and science—the number of women in management has nearly doubled.[15,16] The presence of working women—and working mothers—will be felt at every level of every organization.

Within a few years, more than 40 percent of the workforce will be mothers. If the annual increase in the number of working mothers continues at the same rate, as is likely, more than 80 percent of all mothers with children at home will work.[17] For the last ten years, a majority of mothers of preschool children (six and under) and two-thirds of mothers of school-age children have worked.[18,19]

Domestic Care's Many Faces

Domestic care includes child care, elder care, care for the ill, and care for the temporarily or permanently disabled, as well as the day-to-day chores of supporting a household. Employees can find themselves unexpectedly facing new or increased domestic caregiving responsibilities. A spouse can die or become unable to work, breaking down the family support system and adding a new challenge. A domestic partner can fall ill. A spouse can be promoted, and the more demanding assignment can thereby increase the domestic load on the other. Since serious competition between work and domestic care can burden almost any employee, it is an issue for every employee.

Customary in discussions of the workforce is reference to conflicts between work and family, and it is pointless to defy the terminology. However, the term *family* is too narrow if it only covers a legally recognized union of man, woman, and children under the same roof. According to the 1990 census, about 8 percent of households are nontraditional. Also, a young worker can live alone and still care for elders. With respect to employee stress and productivity, any of these relationships can produce home/work conflicts equivalent to those generated by an "orthodox" family.

Note that flexibility is not an employee benefit but a mutually agreed work arrangement. Its use by nontraditional families is distinct from, for example, the debate over access to health benefits to an unrelated domestic partner. Flexible managers do not define family; employees do that on their own time and in their own ways. Rather, flexible managers manage work in a way that empowers employees to better manage nonwork.[20]

Still, no manager gains by disregarding or ignoring the reality that care-giving competes with working. Attending a domestic partner with AIDS, housing and helping a newly arrived immigrant relative, or meeting with the teachers of a troubled progeny are everyday, everywhere commitments in this society.

Care-giving to children or elders is a burden unevenly distributed between men and women. While men accept that work will interfere with their family roles, the reverse is traditional for women, for whom nonwork responsibilities intrude on work life.[21] Women in families who work at least thirty hours a week also spend more than four hours a day caring for their families.[22] They spend twenty hours per week providing elder care, compared to twelve hours per week spent by men. Indisputably, women put in more hours care-giving than their husbands and perceive greater work/family conflicts as a result.[23]

Elder Care

Elder care issues are gaining recognition as the population, overall, lives longer. Still, they are even more neglected than child care issues. As of 1991, some 5,500 companies had some kind of child care program, while only 300 had an elder care program in place.[24] Yet workers who have elder care commitments may be as many as one in four.[25] The American Association of Retired Persons (AARP) claims that 14 percent of elder care–givers switched to part-time work, 12 percent quit altogether, and 28 percent considered quitting because of conflicts between work and elder care.[26] The Family and Work Foundation places a much lower percentage of elder care–givers (7 percent), but also found that elder care will become a commitment for many more.[27]

An internal study by the Travelers Insurance Corporation counted that 20 percent of its workers over thirty devoted, on average, 10.2 hours a week caring for elders, and some spent as much as thirty-five hours a week shopping and cooking for elders, bringing elders to medical appointments, and finding programs to provide elder care to help their elders and themselves.[28,29] IBM says its internal study showed that 30 percent of its workers care for elders.[30] One elderly man at a cancer center ruefully told the staff how his daughter had used up her entire year's worth of vacation taking him to and from appointments. Nationally, absenteeism has increased 100 percent in the last ten years, and one study attributes 37 percent of that increase to elder care.[31] According to Andrew Scharlack, a professor of gerontology at the University of California, Berkeley, lost productivity resulting from time missed and replacing workers who quit because of elder care costs U.S. companies $17 billion a year, or $2,500 per care-giving employee.[32]

Functionally, the demands of elder care can be strikingly similar to those of child care in the conflicts they generate with work life. Often elder care–giving requirements are intermittent, unpredictable, and unavoidable during work hours. Indeed, elder care responsibilities can be quite formidable because community assistance is poorly developed and because preventative, planned medical care gives way to unplanned, urgent, therapeutic care. Hence, the options of flexing a part of a day or telecommuting some portion of the week can be crucial to a worker committed to elder care.

A maturing workforce needs to be managed differently. Increasingly, workers will inherit elder care responsibilities as parents and in-laws also age. Among those who are not already doing so, some 18 percent of workers predict they will be caring for elders.[33] A greater percentage will have child-care responsibilities. More and more families with have *both*, putting them in the so-called sandwich generation.

The Bottom Line

As early as 1977, 38 percent of working men and 43 percent of working women reported trouble with home and work conflicts.[34] Today, 66 percent of working women experience some difficulty balancing home and work and 20 percent describe it as difficult. A whopping 80 percent of women feel stress or anxiety as a result of home/work conflicts.[35] One woman in ten has left a job because of the struggle, and another 14 percent have considered quitting.[36] A 1991 Gallup Poll reported that 43 percent of employed women expect to reduce their job commitments in the next five years.[37] While they may not do so for economic reasons, it is inconceivable that tensions that make women think about quitting their jobs or cutting back their hours don't take a toll on their day-to-day work life.

Statistics, granted, are hard to follow, easy to forget. They pale before beliefs extracted from personal experience. Yet personal experience is not always a reliable source of management philosophy. Frankly, many managers live quite differently than many of their employees. Executives may generalize from their own traditional family structures to those they manage, even though their lifestyles are quite different.[38] As a result, their assumptions about how well employees arbitrate conflicts between work and nonwork can be inaccurate.[39]

The personnel research organization Bureau of National Affairs (better known as BNA) bluntly contends that many corporations are run by men who have stay-at-home wives and who have not grasped the problem of balancing work and family.[40] An internal study of Corning employees found that 80 percent of those in traditional, single-income families were men in upper management. Employees, quite fairly, often perceive management as lacking empathy with employee conflicts between work and family.[41]

These statistics make clear that the modern worker juggles work and family as never before. Predictions of the productivity, performance, and absenteeism of today's employee must take into account the impact of conflicting demands from work and nonwork on his or her day.

Work/Family Conflicts, a Management Issue

Conflicts between home and work, especially those that revolve around care-giving, are widely publicized, frequently discussed, and hardly news to managers. Institutions are increasingly goaded to come to terms with the changing workforce. A 1992 BNA study determined that of 400 companies surveyed about their maternity, paternity, infant care, and adoption policies, half had changed those policies in the previous five years.[42]

An impressive list of companies have chosen flexibility as their response. For example, the Merck Corporation, the world's largest pharmaceutical manufacturer, enthusiastically implements flexible work, explaining that the desire for improved productivity requires action to minimize potential stress between work and personal life.[43]

Nonetheless, if it were plain to managers that flexible work arrangements effectively support conflicted care-givers, and provide tangible benefits to the organizations sponsoring them, flexibility would enjoy wide currency. Despite two decades of talk, organized management programs to ease home and work conflicts remain highly controversial and somewhat scarce.

The root cause of the controversy at a policy level is that the vast majority of employers are unconvinced that personal issues should factor into managing human resources, or, if they are, they should be factored negatively. In the first instance, they wall off an employee's life after the workday from the scope of their interests. They may argue that official recognition of employee personal life is intrusive.

In the second instance, deplorably, many companies do not ignore work/home conflicts and leave employees to them sort out, but instead treat conflicts with family as bona fide liabilities.[44] Unwritten rules such as "Never bring family concerns to the office" or "Put in long hours regardless of family responsibilities" continue to separate work and family.[45]

When that separation is reduced because a worker goes on maternity leave or an employee is perceived as distracted because a worker is a known parent, careers are sometimes adversely affected. For example, unpaid paternity leaves are rarely taken by men who can afford them because they believe parental leave takers are viewed unfavorably by management, regardless of official policies and the recently passed federal Family Leave Act.[46]

A survey of the Women in Management organization found that 30 percent of married women respondents, with or without children, felt their careers were hurt because they were seen as less available to their employers whether or not they were. Forty-one percent of women managers with small children felt that becoming a parent hurt their careers, not necessarily because parenting vied for extra hours (although for some it did), but because motherhood was presumed to lessen organizational commitment. It is a prophecy which becomes self-fulfilling.[47] For instance, women managers complained of having to prove themselves all over again when returning from maternity leave, as if they had become less able simply because they had given birth.[48]

Through telecommuting programs the state of California found that its agencies could retain the expertise and services of women during pregnancy and during the first four months of infant-rearing, provide them income, and keep them actively engaged in their work.[49] At stake is not only continuity of income, but as one mother put it, "The frustration of being unable to keep current [in her field] . . . and feelings of being reduced to a three-year-old's mentality" when at home with baby and without work.[50]

Flextime, as Table 3–1 demonstrates, can also make a big difference. It assists with resolving work/family conflicts, especially for women. As well, flextime improves an employee's ability to use car pools, take care of personal business, and even find time for recreation.

Flexible management, interested in conserving productivity, implements policies to reduce conflicts with care-giving. Flexible management is more equitable than other organizational programs that reduce work/family conflicts, as it can be extended equally to women and men, to single and married employers, to leisure seekers, to managers, professionals, classified employees—even to those on assembly lines, in police cars, or hospitals.

Strategies for Managing Work/Family Conflicts

Some 5,500 companies have established programs to reduce work/family conflicts. These programs fall into four categories:

TABLE 3-1

Survey Results: Resolving Role-Conflict Issues Through Flextime

	Employees on Flextime (%)	Employees on Rigid Schedules (%)	Difference (%)
I find car-pooling arrangements:			
a. very difficult to arrange	6.6	8.3	-1.7
b. difficult to arrange	6.6	36.7	-30.1
c. easy to arrange	60.0	43.3	-16.7
d. very easy to arrange	26.8	11.7	15.1
Making arrangements for childcare during the workweek is:			
a. very difficult	0.0	0.0	0.0
b. difficult	3.8	20.0	-16.2
c. easy	46.2	33.3	12.9
d. very easy	50.0	46.7	3.3
My opportunities to spend time with my family during the workweek are:			
a. very inadequate	2.0	3.2	-1.2
b. inadequate	2.0	24.2	-22.2
c. adequate	69.4	67.7	1.7
d. very adequate	26.5	4.8	21.7
My opportunities for taking care of my personal business during the workweek are:			
a. very inadequate	2.0	9.7	-7.7
b. inadequate	2.0	27.4	-25.4
c. adequate	57.1	51.6	5.5
d. very adequate	38.8	11.3	27.5
My opportunities for off-the-job recreation during the workweek are:			
a. very inadequate	4.6	1.7	2.9
b. inadequate	2.3	18.3	-16.0
c. adequate	53.5	56.7	-3.2
d. very adequate	39.5	23.3	16.2

Source: Ralston, 1990.

time-based programs such as flextime, job-sharing, part-time work alternatives, and reduced hours; attachment-based programs such as pregnancy and childbirth leave, leave for care of very young children, parental leave, sabbaticals, and telecommuting (where the employee changes the attachment to the workplace); assistance programs such as referrals, inventories of community resources, and in some cases, capitalization or charitable support of community care-giving resources; and provisioning of child care in-house, by subsidies, or by diversion of pre-tax earnings.[51] Of 3,700 companies surveyed who have work/family programs, about 1,500 provide financial assistance, 600 run in-house child-care programs, and 1,600 provide information, and about the same number allow flexible work arrangements, allow emergency child-care leave, or permit employee-elected redirection of accumulated sick time to care for others.

While a scientific economic comparison of flexible work arrangements to its alternatives is not available—research has yet to be done—some assessment of relative benefit, employer-cost, and effectiveness is possible. On the whole, flexible work arrangements are the least expensive to both the employer and the employee.[52] As Chapter 8 discusses in detail, the direct costs of flextime and telecommuting are small, even where organizations must invest in technologies, expand telecommunication networks, or pay for the overhead of managing by objective. Many of these costs are balanced by productivity gains, savings in space utilization, and reduced absenteeism. By contrast, employer-sponsored, in-house day care has a "mixed reputation" in measures of satisfaction, productivity gains, or reduced absenteeism.[53] Employers need not attempt to justify flexible work arrangements as good citizenship or as exercises in social-responsibility.[54] They can make a hard dollar case for starting a flexible work program.

Flexible Work, Women, and Child Care

Since child-care conflicts are so common among employees, the debate about the employer's role in resolving them has spiraled over the years. In the first half of the 1980s, flexible work was widely proclaimed as the solution to child-care problems.[55] Lanier Business Products published an infamous advertisement showing a contented mother juggling a baby in one hand and business equipment in the other.[56] In 1983, Congressman Newt Gingrich unsuccessfully promoted tax abatements for computers purchased for home businesses as a child-care solution (among other considerations). *Newsweek* proclaimed in 1984 that a new era was beginning where "Mom" would balance children and job by working at home.[57] Throughout the 1980–1985 period, many popularizers of telecommuting claimed working from home would solve the child-care dilemma.

In 1985, a Traveler's Insurance program for retaining former employees as contract programmers was idealized for mothers of young children and as a way for companies to take advantage of well-trained employees who had left their jobs. The company, losing women programmers to child bearing and child raising, developed a terrific backlog of projects to finish. The solution was a telecommuting program . . . "It's been very advantageous to us to work with former employees, trained by us, who know our way of doing business," said . . . [an] information services training manager.[58] However, many work-at-home arrangements failed because the double burdens of work and care of young children proved impossible to manage at either end.[59] A number of scholars, corporate managers, and popularizers were prompted to speak out against home-based work as a child care solution.[60-64] As early as 1985, Patricia Mokhtarian, a civil engineer who studies flexible work, cautioned that telecommuting does not obviate the need for child care.[65]

Nonetheless, many promotions of flexible work clung to the notion that telecommuting could solve child care problems.[66] The telecommuting option was pinned on child-care objectives. Margrethe Olson, New York University's director of studies of home-based work, would suggest that the main engine of the then few flexiplace programs in the United States was the search for child-care solutions for working women.[67] In spite of arguments against the use of telecommuting (full-time home-based work) as a child-care solution, corporate executives would continue to see child care as its most important rationale.[68]

By the end of the decade, the opposition to telecommuting as a child-care program (again, home-based work usually on a full-time basis) became resolute:

"It's a mistake to assume that a person can pursue work involving any level of concentration and take care of preschool children at the same time," says Kathleen Christensen, Director of City University of New York's National Project on Home-based work.[69]

"One fallacy is that if you work at home you don't need child care. That's ridiculous," says [Carl Kirkpatrick, JC Penney's planning and program manager].[70]

Studies showed, indeed, that home-based workers would typically either have child care provided on a fee or voluntary basis while they worked or work only while their children were asleep. They spent more on child care than office-based workers.[71-73] Child advocates argued that the rhetoric of flexible work was being used by some proponents to let employers and the government off the hook of funding child care.[74]

An anomaly developed. On the one hand, decision-makers with authority to implement flexible work often persist in the idea that it supports child care; on the other hand, experience does not support the linkage. The polarization seemingly forces a choice, and led some analysts to reject altogether the domestic-care rationale for flexible work.[75]

The truer formulation lies between. While flexible schedules and telecommuting are not substitutes for child care, flexible work is one recourse among few for women balancing the competing demands of uncompensated domestic work and employment.[76]

Flexible work can help out in various stages of parenting. The pregnant employee flexes time in order to obtain prenatal care and training without absenteeism. Without flexible work options, an employee who needs income while on maternity leave first must use up all accrued sick leave and, then, she becomes eligible for six to eight weeks of disability. This means no more than eight to twelve weeks of paid leave—at less than full pay. For the mother wishing to stay at home longer (or for the father to spend any time home at all), the only alternative is leave without pay. This sequence finds the parent between a rock and a hard place, forced to choose between a rapid return to work bereft of sick leave, or a complete loss of income. In the hardest places, of course, are single-income, single heads of households and those in lower income brackets.

For toddlers and preschool children, paid child care becomes only comparatively more available. There are only 2.5 million child-care slots to greet the 36.2 million children of working parents.[77] Although flexible work does not by itself relieve child care needs or expenses, it assists both parents in making use of paid care by giving them room to maneuver:

> ... A telecommuter may find child care within ten minutes of home, and if the child became ill, it would be relatively easy for the parent to take a ten-minute drive to pick up the youngster. This is in comparison with the difficulty of traveling constantly between three locations— work, home and a day-care center.[78]

The Family and Work Foundation found that 26 percent of employed parents with children under the age of 13 had experienced a breakdown in their usual child-care arrangements in the preceding three months of the survey, and 32 percent of parents of children under age 5 had had a breakdown in child-care arrangements. Flexible work makes these more manageable by allowing employees to stretch the traditional working schedule around other responsibilities so the unpredictable can be handled.[79-81]

Where flexible work is probably most helpful in child care is among parents of school-age children. For them, reliable before-school or after-school care is very difficult to find, and if findable, inconvenient or costly. Taking a few minutes for transporting children to and from school and or checking on their well being while they play do not hurt a parent's ability to work as a telecommuter, but greatly benefit care giving.

Note that the period during which children are "school age" (6 to 18 years old) is more than double that of "pre-school age" (birth to 5 years old). Who has not seen a co-worker tune out in the afternoon waiting for a child to call in to confirm a safe journey home from school? A researcher reports that 48 percent of women and 25 percent of men spend unproductive time at work because of child-care concerns.[82]

In the absence of flexible work scheduling, many families raise latchkey children. An internal study by the Du Pont Corporation determined that 43 percent of their workers' children between ages 10 and 13 were routinely alone after school, a figure (42 percent) confirmed by a national 1990 Child Welfare League of America study of latchkey children.[83] This translates into an estimated 8 to 10 million children left alone each weekday before or after school.[84]

Such children, observed a Los Angeles truant officer, are more prone to teenage dysfunctionalities such as gang membership and dropping out of school.[85] Latchkey children watch a lot more television to fill the silence of being alone. Another study found *double* the likelihood of illegal drug use among latchkey children compared to children who were not home alone after school.[86] Because flexible work increases parent/child contact, it could have far-reaching social benefits.

What school-age children, ill children, and others at home need because of infirmity or disability is partial adult oversight and intermittent care.[87] Yet, without flexibility, too many employees must spend ten or more consecutive hours commuting and working each day. Flextime and telecommuting combinations help structure caregiving activities so they are more consistent with full-time employment. Some telecommuters will shift work duty from the after-school period to the evening. Others will simply let their children check in, more secure in the knowledge that a bruised knee can get a bandage and a teary eye can get wiped.

Employers who worry that they will end up paying for their workers to say home to provide child care need to reevaluate their assumptions. According to BNA, forty-eight hours a year are missed by workers as a result of short-term child care urgencies and emergencies such as school closings because of weather, medical appointments, or short-term childhood illnesses.[88,89] The Los Angeles Department of Water and Power estimates it spends $1 million a year in salary and benefits because of absenteeism caused by child-care problems.[90]

Time-reporting systems for flextime workers and telecommuters allow employees to accommodate work and emergencies rather than forcing them to choose. The flextime workers will bank additional time the next day, for example, or the telecommuter will give over additional time in the evening. In traditional arrangements, the employee's only recourses are to feign illness, become tardy, or take vacation time taken with little notice to the employer. The traditional employer pays by financing absenteeism, but can never recover the cost of absent employees.

Conclusion

Flexibility in work is economical and empowering; it responds to diversity. With a permanent labor shortage and a changing demographic and gender profile of workers, flexibility is the only long-term strategy known to conserve labor resources and improve productivity.

Despite the blind eye turned by many traditional managers, the costs and effects of work/family conflicts riddle organizations of every size. Although flexible work arrangements do not replace child-care arrangements, in-house care for the elderly, or other direct care-giving, they allow employees to balance work and family. As employees better manage their own lives, employers can better manage them.

Already, flexible work arrangements have proved their usefulness in recruiting and retaining workers, in reducing expensive and wasteful absenteeism, and in responding to the realities of the modern lifestyle.

4

The Benefits of Flexible Work

E very organization in America is looking for ways to be more
productive, attract and retain better employees, improve customer service, mend the environment and comply with air quality
regulations and aspirations, and alleviate the consequences of disasters. Flexible work arrangements offer all of these advantages and
others to your organization.

Productivity

As Jim Manzi, a manager with the Lotus Development Corporation, put it, "office productivity is like pornography. You can't define it, but you know it when you see it."[1] Productivity is difficult to
define, much less measure, especially for professional staff. Objective measures of changes in productivity can be even more elusive
when workers move from project to project. There is no obvious
way to compare the time required to complete different projects,
or their relative quality. Studies of telecommuter productivity
sometimes rely on poor definitions that measure only output/unit
of time worked, ignoring other measures of productivity including
quality of work, more efficient coordination with colleagues, and
reduced absenteeism.[2]

Thus, many of the reported gains in productivity in flexible work
programs are anecdotal or based on subjective assessments of managers or telecommuters. However, there are instances where it is

51

possible to meter the productivity gains telecommuters realize, namely, among those whose output can be readily quantified—such as data-entry clerks, computer programmers, word processors, and others who generate enumerable units of output. For these flexible workers, productivity gains are certifiable:

- The Control Data Corporation reports a 15 to 25 percent improvement in productivity among at-home programmers "in terms of on-time delivery, goals met, and goals improved upon."[3]
- Telecommuting programmers in the Traveler's Insurance Company's flexible work program were said to increase productivity by 22 percent.[4]
- Telecommuting programmers and system support personnel at Aetna Life and Casualty "routinely complete their tasks 25 percent faster than their full-time office worker counterparts."[5]
- Telecommuting data-entry clerks in a department of Los Angeles County experienced a 37 percent increase in productivity; the gain was even greater if their 60 percent fewer entry errors are taken into account.[6]
- Corning Glass showed a 5 percent increased in productivity among workers on compressed work weeks.
- In a study of a telecenter, data entry improved by 10 percent over nontelecenter productivity, and there was a 50 percent improvement in planning efficiency, a gain that eliminated the need for overtime.[7]
- Twenty-four managerial telecommuters at New York Telephone reported a 43 percent gain in productivity.[8]
- International Computers Limited, a British company, claims that a telecommuter working at home can accomplish in twenty-five hours what it takes an office-bound worker forty hours to do.[9]

While the "transferability" of these data to others kinds of professional and clerical work may be speculative, they are consistent with subjective ratings of productivity gains among telecommuting professionals:

- In a survey of executives in companies sponsoring telecommuting, 94 percent reported an increase in productivity and 52 percent reported that quality of output increased; 57 percent also reported improved morale.[10]

- In the telecommuting pilot at the Southern California Association of Governments (SCAG), "the great majority of managers rated their employees 'more productive' while telecommuting . . . Almost every manager felt that 'less time' was required for staff persons to produce the same type of work and, significantly, every manager rated the quality of work produced either 'about equal' or 'higher' than before."[11]
- A British study of telecommuting found that telecommuting causes actual work output to rise by 20 percent to 30 percent per person per week.[12]
- A purchasing department coordinator for Volusia County (Deland, Florida) claimed a 300 percent workload increase was handled due to telecommuting without staff increases and said his own productivity jumped 50 percent when working at home freed him from interruptions.[13]
- A project manager, Don Rouse, with British Columbia Telephone Company, says workers at a neighborhood work center who had cut a ninety-minute commute to a few minutes "hit the door ready to work, rather than ready to rest. Some people in the company feel productivity has improved as much as 25 percent." One job trainer produced twelve courses in the center compared to nine in the same time period in the office.[14]

Some argue that telecommuters accomplish more than their office-bound counterparts only by working more hours, not by getting more done in the same amount of time. They may work longer (uncompensated) hours because they have more work than a supplementer can stuff in a briefcase and carry home, and they have the space and equipment set up to handle it. However, regardless of whether employees are more productive or just working longer hours when telecommuting, most managers will welcome the results as a productivity gain. Many professional employees are expected to work hours consistent with the requirements of their position and they are informally allowed to flex schedules to accommodate the cyclical workload generated by their assignments.

The most consistent explanation for productivity gains found in evaluations of telecommuting brings one back to the reason people have long taken work home: the office is an intrusive, unproductive environment for cognitive activities such as reading, writing, analyzing, computing, editing, designing, data input, and the like. Ultimately, it may be that flexible work does not increase productivity so much as office work decreases it! The communication-related benefits of office life—easy access to co-workers, spontaneous meetings, "just a quick question" interruptions—all conspire against the tasks of many jobs.[15] Personnel planners assume that at least a paid hour each day in the office exclusive of authorized breaks is completely unproductive.

Additional productivity factors include the conversion of commuting time to work time, faster access to mainframe computer services during offpeak periods (lowered contention for CPU and I/O services), and work schedules customized to an individual's bioclock.[16]

A memorandum from a telecommuter, a data processing supervisor at a University of California, Davis telecommunications department, provides a classic illustration of how telecommuting may improve productivity and free up an employee's life in a single stroke.

> In anticipation of the Administrative Billing Closing, there were about nine files that needed to be processed. [Technically,] there is no way these files could be processed if I did this within the confines of 8–5 P.M., Monday–Friday.
>
> Friday evening, I dialed up and started the process for one file; it took about five minutes of my time. Saturday A.M. I dialed from home and began the next one . . .
>
> If I did not have my home terminal, although each [file] required less than ten minutes, I would have had to make four trips from home . . . an hour of commute and work time. The campus "call back" policy says a minimum of three hours of compensatory time is recorded for each return to the workplace. So, by this interpretation I would have "earned" twelve hours of compensatory time to do what took less than a half-hour total from my home.[17]

Of course, not all tasks work so well remotely, but when they can, the effects are excellent.

Not all gains in productivity resulting from flexible work are output-related; they may, instead, refer to improvements in the quality of work. An analyst for Merrill Lynch describes how many fellow analysts were aggressively touting automobile stocks. A long-distance telecommuter based in San Francisco, this analyst remained negative and, in fact, auto stocks slid 30 percent not long thereafter. The analyst doubted he could have "resisted the bullishness" had he been working on Wall Street. There, "you have the herd instinct operating . . . You have salesmen and traders sitting right next to the analysts saying Maryann Keller's recommending them and she's smart . . . Elain Garzarelli's recommending them and she's smart . . ."[18] By working independently, this trader was able to retain his objectivity.

Absenteeism

Absenteeism is a growing problem for all employers—and for the national economy. For every one-half-percent increase in U.S. absenteeism, the gross national product declines by some $10 billion annually.[19] As cited earlier, hours lost to absenteeism has doubled in the last ten years. To put the level of absentee hours in perspective, it is equivalent to a 40 percent increase in the unemployment rate. In 1986, the *Wall Street Journal* estimated that a day's absence of a clerical worker costs, in addition to wages, "up to $100 in reduced efficiency and increased supervisory workload."[20] A carefully done study of a flextime program concluded that workers are more often absent because they are unable to come to work than because they are not motivated to work. Family care emergencies, minor illnesses, and personal appointments that must be scheduled during the day account for unplanned absences.[21]

Both flextime and telecommuting reliably reduce absenteeism:

- A former Pacific Bell executive says that employees at the company's southern California satellite work centers have a rate of absenteeism 25 percent lower than those that work in the downtown Los Angeles location.[22]
- In the state of California telecommuting pilot project, sick time reported by telecommuters was also 25 percent less than non-telecommuters.[23] In fact, the reduction in absenteeism is one of the factors leading the pilot's consultant to estimate a 7-to-1 return on the telecommuting program costs of about $125,000 over two years.[24]
- A study of flextime at Blue Cross documented a decline in sick

days reported from an average of eight hours per month to 2.3 hours per month.[25]

- Another study comparing different kinds of flextime with un-flexed schedules found absenteeism reduced in all kinds of flexible scheduling, although it was lowest among those working "staggered fixed schedules."[26]

In perhaps the most careful study of the impact of flextime on absenteeism, researchers Dalton and Mesch were able to examine the behavior of employees at a "natural laboratory." At one factory, flextime was implemented for one group of workers, but not for another. Furthermore, the flextime program was experimental and was terminated after it became conflict-ridden in disputes with the local union. Thus, it was possible to see both the change in absenteeism in one group depending on flextime options and compare that change with workers sticking to traditional shifts. As the figure shown illustrates, the results were dramatic.

Part of the reason flextime and telecommuting (combined with flextime) reduce absenteeism is that they permit employees to break out of the work day for short periods for medical appointments or for other personal reasons which otherwise require that they use sick time. Sometimes a telecommuter uses a lunch hour to schedule a medical appointment while working from home, while the distance to doctor would be prohibitive if that individual were working in the office.[27] Telecommuting also reduces absenteeism by allowing contagious employees to work at home rather than to come to the office where they might infect co-workers. Indeed, one study estimates a 6-percent reduction in workplace illness if those with contagions such as the common cold worked from home.[28]

There may also be a reduction in stress-related illness and consequent absenteeism among flexible workers who feel less need to take "mental health days" or who do not experience severe stress requiring leaves.[29] Work-related stress is the most frequent disability claim (especially among women workers), so the relief of stress has economic value.

Telecommuting also contributes to reduced absenteeism among the temporarily disabled. A variety of illnesses and other temporary physical disabilities are severe enough to prevent a worker from

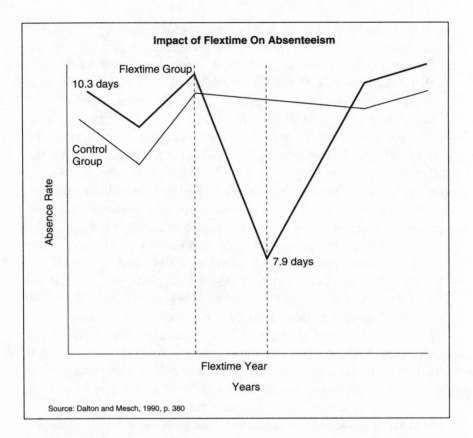

Impact of Flextime On Absenteeism

Flextime Group
10.3 days

Control
Group

Absence Rate

7.9 days

Flextime Year

Years

Source: Dalton and Mesch, 1990, p. 380

coming into an office, but are not so severe that the worker could not work from home. Short-term telecommuting (for those who are not already regular telecommuters) can reduce sick days and the organizational impact of the worker's absence.[30] In one company, a secretary worked full-time from home as she recuperated from a broken hip once her disability payments were exhausted.[31] Some companies maintain loaner computers specifically for use by the temporarily disabled such as those on maternity leave. (Note: There are some liability concerns about telecommuting performed by the temporarily disabled.)

Customer Service

Sometimes relatively simple flextime arrangements can improve productivity by increasing service levels to customers. Flextime is an important kind of flexible work because it is used by employees who cannot, given the nature of their jobs, telecommute.

For example, the compressed work week (nine-hour work days, with a day off every other week) was begun by a team of technicians at a telecommunications company. On regular shifts, installers and repair personnel would start work at 8:00 A.M.; their first half hour on the job was spent loading trucks with equipment, reviewing the day's work orders, and organizing routes and partners. Similarly, the last half hour of the day (4:30 P.M.–5:00 P.M.) was spent unloading the trucks of equipment that wasn't to be left vulnerable to theft in the parking lot, turning in work order slips of completed jobs, and discussing issues with the foreman that arose during the day.

When they went to nine hour days (with a day off every other week) the same hour was adequate to set-up and set-down the day's work. The result was that instead of spending 5 x 7 = 35 hours/week installing and repairing, they spent 5 x 8 = 40 hours/week at this billable activity, a productivity improvement of 12.5 percent *per worker*. Bigger jobs were finished faster, and short-notice jobs could be handled more readily. Aside from the minor overhead of planning coverage and scheduling alternating compressed days off, there was no additional cost to the employer even though they were working fewer days per month.

A natural gas company surveyed customers and found the standard work day was a source of complaints. By introducing flextime, the company was able to offer after-hour service to customers and provide its employees greater schedule flexibility without increased head count, overtime pay, or increased benefit costs.[32] In this "win, win, win," situation, customers, employees, and the company all gained from the flexible arrangement.

Morale and Job Satisfaction

One of the reasons flexible working improves productivity is that it improves employee morale and job satisfaction; people who like their working conditions predictably work harder, better, and longer.[33] In a study of home-based telecommuting, participants reported that they felt "more in control of their lives . . . that they were better able to concentrate on crucial tasks, had lower feelings of work-related stress, and were able to get significantly more done."[34] In a sense, flexible work is a means to realizing a greater return on personnel dollars through the productivity gains that greater job satisfaction accrues.[35] However, satisfied employees are also cost-avoiders: they claim less worker's compensation and take fewer sick days.

As previously discussed, circumspection is essential in evaluating the impact of flexible work on care-giving. Nonetheless, it can obviously reduce schedule conflicts between the personal and work lives of employees. This, in turn, helps employees to focus on their jobs as they perform them rather than on their family responsibilities. It also reduces diversion of sick leave for family care purposes.

Flextime can work as well as telecommuting to increase job satisfaction.[36,37] A data-entry clerk at a large company was terribly frustrated by an overworked computer system that slowed down to a crawl because it was too small for the number of users it supported. She changed her starting time from eight to four in the morning. In the otherwise empty office the computer was lightning fast; her productivity soared as the computer kept up with her; in the quiet early morning atmosphere, she was able to concentrate; her job satisfaction zoomed.

Her overlap with the standard workday was adequate to allow her to coordinate her work with others in her group. This is important, since reports are mixed regarding intraoffice coordination among those working flextime schedules. Some observers find teamwork encouraged because flextimer workers have to exert more effort at coordination while others find projects delayed for the same reason.[38,39]

Bioclocks

The importance of individual bioclocks, personal cycles of energy and fatigue, may sound like new age fluff, but to anyone who works alone on projects, it is palpable. Russ Monbleau, a recruiting manager for the Digital Equipment Corporation, explains:

> With a [telecommuting] system at home, I can work at 6 A.M., at midnight, or on weekends, without getting into the car and driving to the office—and then feeling like I am committed for a least a few hours because I have burned a couple of hours in the car.[40]

In fact, most telecommuters also work flextime schedules; managers who work with telecommuters become accustomed to electronic mail or voice mail composed at odd hours. At the John Hancock Insurance Company flextime for telecommuters could be anytime:

> Telecommuting has proven itself to be a flexible work style that fits perfectly with creative workers . . . "The people with whom I work are creative types," said Mr. Malcolm [Director of Strategic Services]. "They don't start thinking at 8:30 in the morning, nor do they stop thinking at 4:30 in the afternoon. Some of the best work probably is done in the wee hours of the morning or late at night."[41]

One company urges telecommuters to keep their telephone bills down by dialing-up computer services during the less expensive night telephone rate periods. Working very late at the office is eerie for anyone; women telecommuters in particular may find that working according to their bioclocks feels safer than being in a barren office late at night or taking mass transit at lonely hours. Employees can manage their own work to improve productivity in ways no employer could.

Avoiding the stress of commuting, improved employee motivation, reduced absenteeism, and supporting the labors of the disabled, the somewhat ill, the pregnant, or the convalescing, all contribute to bottom-line productivity.

Retention and Recruitment

Some companies save money through flexible work programs by recruiting distant employees as telecommuters without necessarily having to relocate them; executive relocation can cost from $25,000 to $50,000.[42] The California State Franchise Tax Board in Sacramento badly wanted to hire an economist who lived happily in San Francisco, a hundred miles from the organization. He took the job as a telecommuter; the Board avoided the cost of relocation and probably would have failed in the recruitment had it insisted that he move. To the extent that employees can be retained because they are satisfied with flexible work arrangements, an additional $20,000 to $25,000 per professional in training and in lower initial productivity could also be saved. One study estimates that a 12 percent turnover in a company of 500 employees costs $600,000 in out-of-pocket recruiting cost, retraining, and productivity losses.[43] Government agencies such as the National Science Foundation are using the carrot of telecommuting to attract scientists despite its less-than-competitive salary scale.[44] An insurance company began a program of reinvolving retirees through telecommuting who might be reluctant to rekindle the daily commuter's grind and schedule despite their interest in working.

Employee safety

The commitment to a safe employee environment helps motivate a flexible work program. Consider the oft-repeated speculation that flexible work programs increase employer liability because of the potential for coverable home accidents during scheduled work hours. However, experience indicates that employees are safer at home. On the contrary, the most dangerous time for most employees is when they commute to and from work.

By eliminating commuting or by flexing the time of commute, transportation dangers can be measurably decreased. According to Arthur Schiller of the consulting firm Arthur D Little, if 12 percent of the work force were to telecommute only one day a week, the result would be *1.6 million fewer accidents* and *1,100 fewer traffic-related deaths annually*.[45] Notwithstanding the fact that workers' compensation does not cover commuter injuries, lost time deprives organizations of staff and thereby incurs costs. The reduction of commute-related traffic accidents is a valid economic objective.

Some observers opine that telecommuting, if widely practiced, might reduce the threat of neighborhood crime by repopulating deserted bedroom communities during the day. On the other hand, one prominent consultant warns telecommuters to keep their computers away from windows so as not to attempt burglars! Perhaps when home computers become as common as telephones they'll be less attractive to criminals.

Disaster Mitigation

During California's major earthquakes in 1990 and 1993 many companies established remote work centers and telecommuting arrangements because arterial damage made commuting untenable for many employees. In the aftermath of the Los Angeles earthquake, the City of Los Angeles and Pacific Bell set up a special agency to assist companies trying to use telecommuting to end run transportation chaos. In Florida, employees who lost their homes in the 1993 hurricanes became telecommuters at the homes of friends and relatives who took them in. Employees at the World Trade Center worked from home and remote offices after the building was bombed and closed for repairs. A Texas newspaper allowed writers to telecommute. After it burned to the ground in 1992, it borrowed presses from another paper and coordinated writers and reporters by telephone; its prior experience with telecommuting helped the work flow smoothly during the crisis.

Studies of the 1990 Loma Prieta earthquake in San Francisco showed that companies who had telecommuting programs in place before the disaster struck were significantly less affected by the commuter crisis it created than those who attempted telecommuting on the fly, when their staffs could not come to work as they normally would. This earthquake forced closure of eleven transportation structures (bridges, overpasses, raised freeways, including the bridge connecting the East Bay and San Francisco).[46] Flexible work, especially telecommuting, carries the side benefit that it helps prepare for the disruption of work due to disasters such as earthquakes, floods, fires, highway construction, office relocation, epidemic, or civil disorder.[47]

Environmental Benefits

Regulations of large employers (more than 100 employees) increasingly oblige government organizations and businesses to alleviate transportation and environmental problems created by the large commuter population. Even in regions that have yet to experience congestive traffic failure, traffic is becoming a major issue because of commuter frustration and air quality management. The deluge of traffic and its greatest tributary, single-passenger vehicles carrying commuters to and from work, will only be abated by a combination of strategies from car pooling and mass transit to telecommuting and remote work locations.[48,49] Given the high cost of mass transit, regions are forcing employers to accept the onus of commute reduction.

Particular stress has been placed on improving the *modal split*, that is, the distribution of tripmaking by car, bus, bicycle, or foot among others.[50] The idea is to move people out of their individual car commutes and into other forms of transportation. County governments in congested areas of California, for example, often require in-county institutions to survey their employees about their transportation modes and ridesharing behavior, and will eventually mandate reduced single-occupied vehicle (SOV) commutes.

From a legal point of view, the reason for the interest is new air quality legislation which migrated from state to state and is now federal law. The Federal Clean Air Act of 1990 mandates specified regions throughout the United States to implement what the federal Environmental Protection Agency calls the Employee Commute Options Program. However, a better name would be the employee SOV abatement program.

EPA mandates specify ways in which states will require employers to reduce solo commuting by car. Companies must implement programs to meet target reductions relative to solo commuting in the region as a whole. For example, if a company in Nassau County, a suburb of New York, has 500 employers, on average 155 of those 500 must stop (or not start) solo commuting in their cars at the time New York regional regulations go into effect.[51]

Telecommuting along with sizable vanpools (six passengers or more), mass transit, bicycling, alternative fuel vehicles, and walking are the most compliant alternatives for companies. If in the example above one employee in six telecommutes two days a week, the goal is met. Affected organizations will use a mix of strategies for compliance; telecommuting is among them. Eventually, companies who do not comply will face financial penalties; in New York, noncompliance can cost an offender a maximum of $500 per day of default; in Connecticut, however, it can cost a company or public institution ten times more, as much as $5,000 a day.[52]

Flextime has been shown to increase the use of mass transit. With a flexible schedule, workers can put up with bus delays without worrying about being tardy. They are also attracted to the smaller crowds at offpeak times which make it more likely that they will find a seat.[53] However, there are severe limitations on the reach of alternative modes of transportation. Car pools are hard to organize, bus routes, especially for people commuting from suburb to suburb or city to suburb are generally impractical or nonexistent, and train and trolley systems are fantastically expensive to build and operate. For the vast majority of Americans, staying put is the alternative to travel by automobile.[54] For that reason, air quality managers and transportation planners are actively pushing telecommuting, the simplest and potentially most popular way to leave the car in the garage and still get to work.

Since the energy crisis of the 1970s, considerable research has explored the potential of telecommunications to substitute for transportation. More recently, it is understood that beginning with the invention of the telegraph, telecommunication sometimes competes with and sometimes abets demand for transportation.[55] For example, the flight of a jumbo jet from New York to London requires transmission of 37,000 electronic messages. At the same time, as early as 1973 it was demonstrated that a fifth of rush hour work trips in the San Francisco area could be replaced by moving ideas electronically rather than people physically.[56] Such estimates pinned their conclusions on the widespread use of teleconferencing—electronic meetings—a technology application which to this day is promoted well and used little.[57]

Now, flexible work—telecommuting and flextime—is kindling a new interest in the many-sided relation between telecommunications and transportation. The moving of work to the worker, electronically, is a decided substitute to moving the worker to his or her work. One sees signs of a "footloose production system transformed by telecommunications."[58] For example, jobs are routinely exported to Taiwan, Barbados, and the Philippines via telecommunications networks—the ultimate remote work centers.[59] Comparatively, it should be simple to move employee tasks to his or her residence for telecommuting purposes.

The need to moderate commuting by automobile is a forceful argument for flexible work. Telecommuting mitigates traffic congestion and improves air quality, as a rigorous study of a telecommuting pilot showed. Commute trips were reduced and nonwork trips did not increase.[60] Telecommuters, on average, cut their weekly commuter miles by about 11 percent.[61] For every 20,000 workers with twenty-mile commutes (low-end commuter miles), telecommuting three days a week would save 12.5 million gallons of gasoline, about three days worth of OPEC oil imports!

With respect to transportation demand management, the good case that telecommuting and flextime are the only realistic ways to accomplish major reductions in commuter traffic has been made for some time:

> A 1978 urban mass transit study indicated that a large shift to alternative work hours would be the easiest, most cost effective, and most appealing strategy to implement to reduce peak-period congestion and air pollution problems.[62]

As employees find themselves pushed out farther away from their jobs because of high housing costs, the public and personal costs of commuting will correspondingly jump.

Flextime doesn't have much environmental impact unless it is a formal program directly associated with reducing the demand for transportation. However, if it is officially sanctioned as a commuter program, flextime is at once the flexible work program most easily implemented on a large scale and the least difficult to manage.

Interestingly, flextime improves smog control by increasing the speed at which drivers commute:

> The reduction in peak-period congestion associated with staggered work hour programs can actually diminish vehicle emissions of smog-causing hydrocarbons (current statistics indicate increasing average freeway speeds from 30 to 55 mph can cut smog by up to 40 percent).[63]

Unlike other alternatives to the single-passenger car used in the daily commute, flextime works well for those who must (or feel they must) bring themselves to work by automobile.

Telecommuting also promotes more efficient use of existing transportation capacity and delays the need to construct expensive new infrastructure by letting people use the excess capacity in the transportation system at offpeak times and places.[64,65] Certainly, the same is true of flextime, especially in tandem with telecommuting.[66]

As mass transit costs go up, the economics of flexible work becomes more inviting. For example, the transportation investment in new roads, road widening, subways, commuter rail, and bus services required to maintain 1988 levels of traffic congestion in northern Virginia was estimated at $10 billion over two decades. In the metropolitan area, this extrapolated to a cost of $25,500 per additional commuting worker, or $2.88 billion altogether to take in account work force growth for just one year. Even a mere 1-percent reduction in physical commutes because of telecommuting is worth $580 million in public capital and ongoing transit subsidies. As former President Bush said in a speech about telecommuting, "not a bad deal."

Conclusion

There is little doubt that flexible work improves productivity even if there continues to be debate about exactly why it does. Resources such as space and mainframe computers can often be effectively expanded at little or no cost by using flextime and telecommuting to reduce contention for space or computer time.

Telecommuting, in particular, seems to improve the work of both professionals and clerical workers. Generally, improved morale and job satisfaction among flexible workers has improved the quality and quantity of their products.

Flexible work arrangements have been used successfully to bolster recruitment and retention of valuable employees, increase hours of customer service, improve employee safety, and even help mitigate the effects of disasters.

Perhaps the biggest economic payback of flexible work is in reduced absenteeism, a horrific expense that has skyrocketed over the last decade. Flexible workers are absent less, use less sick time, and therefore return more value to their employers for their expense.

Governments as well as companies are turning to flexible work to reduce the smog generated by automobile commutes with promising consequences. Although this benefit is tied to participation rates, extrapolations show that even modest amounts of telecommuting and flextime arrangement would help the atmospheric environment and make better use of existing transportation infrastructure.

Despite the hesitations of many employers to implement significant flexible work programs, those employers willing to innovate reap solid economic rewards for their efforts.

5

Challenges to Flexible Work

F lexible work is a paradox. Over the last fifteen years, there has been a dramatic increase in media, government, business, and employee interest in flexible work. New organizations regularly set up flexible work programs. A range of flexible work benefits— from boosting productivity and morale to helping the American family—have been scientifically demonstrated. However, the actual number of flexible workers remains a relatively small percentage of the U.S. workforce. Programs are often in place but managers and supervisors aver. They accept flexible work arrangements slowly or not at all.

A longitudinal study of flextime (through 1985) showed a steady increase in corporate and government programs, from 15 percent in 1977 to 22 percent in 1981 to 29 percent in 1985.[1] The U.S. Bureau of Labor Statistics reported in 1986 that 38 percent of government offices and 44 percent of small, private corporations sponsored flextime.[2] And in 1990, a survey by the Conference Board showed that 50 percent of America's 521 largest companies had flextime programs, and 93 percent of them allowed alternative work arrangements such as telecommuting.[3] However, employees actually participating in flextime programs remained relatively constant at 12 percent between 1986 and 1990.[4]

The consulting firm Work/Family Directions organizes family-friendly programs such as child care and flexible work programs for large corporations. They found that even though flexibility programs are officially sanctioned by their client companies, relatively few employees participate because managers resist the change and employees fear adverse career consequences. Flexibility remains an accommodation to a small number of high performers rather than legitimate means of managing the larger work force.[5]

What is true is that the telecommuting concept has a high profile among managers. In one survey of North Carolina executives, for example, 87 percent recognized the term, 57 percent reported exposure to it from media, and 25 percent personally knew of companies which had telecommuting programs.[6] Nonetheless, only 13 percent of their companies allow telecommuting, and they usually restrict working at home to a few special employees on a few afternoons per week.[7]

Although organizational leaders know about telecommuting, and even setting up programs, they are limiting participation. A consultant's report to the city of Toronto could describe many organizations when it found that while the city officially "values its employees, not only as workers, but as people with responsibilities and stresses outside the work environment," its management practices are "not always family friendly."[8] Organizations increasingly rally on paper to reducing work/family conflicts, but in practice, it's business as usual. In the city of Toronto, as in many U.S. organizations, the gaps between official ideology and management systems are significant.

Gaps will continue so long as flexible work arrangements have the seeming potential to create new difficulties rather than solve problems. If the risks appear high, they will certainly discourage adoption and deter engagement. When organizations decide in favor of flexible work, they must encourage skeptical managers to suspend their suspicions enough to give it a try. The most persuasive approach is to know what can go wrong and how to make sure it doesn't.

Management Resistance

Managerial resistance is the most important barrier to flexible work.[9] Futurist Jack Nilles, often described as the father of telecommuting, concludes that "Management apprehensions about loss of control and unrewarded effort are currently the pacing factors in the adoption of telecommuting."[10] He blames conservative management with industrial revolution mindsets as the major obstacle to telecommuting for the past 15 years.[11]

Nevertheless, the mindset can continue long after it has outlived its relevance. Some managers see working at home as an organizational taboo, a symbolic challenge to the deference owed them. They may believe that remoteness is itself a sign of authority, prestige, and high status which only the employer has the right to control even though telecommuting might be highly productive.[12] They reserve to management the right to travel extensively, to lock one's self up at home to finish a report, or to fiddle with the lunch-hour schedule.[13]

Time and space are used to symbolize status among members of an organization. For example, professionals are not paid for overtime, as a rule, while the Fair Labor Standards Act requires that nonexempt workers must be. Thus, clerical workers are paid for their time, while professionals are paid for their work. Executive offices are often on the top floor of a company building, an implication not only of highest organizational status but of distance from the more mundane concerns taken up on the floors below.[14]

For the manager or supervisor who invests ego in the proximity of his minions, and sees their value only because he controls their schedules, flexible work is especially menacing. The apparent challenge to traditional management control over time and site threatens authority and status.[15] In the 1960s, the well-publicized movement of job restructuring to make jobs more satisfying was routinely obstructed by managers fearful of loosing power and even their station if employees became more autonomous and self-directed.[16]

Although some managers resist flexible work because they are concerned about practicalities of cost, coordination, and frankly, the effort associated with change, managerial opposition wells up from a fear that control over employees will be lost. In research surveys of managers, nearly all negative attitudes towards flexible work are keyed to this reservation.[17] Managers ask, in effect, "if you can't see them, how do you know what they are doing?" Reluctant managers typically associate loss of control with difficulty in monitoring the job performance of remote workers. Managers worry that flexible work prevents effective communications with and among their staff. They believe, underneath, that a loss of control will haunt their own performance records. Like the many employees who are afraid to request flexible arrangements, they too are bound by fear.

Managers relate concerns about the availability of staff (for quick resolution of unexpected problems or for unplanned meetings). To a lesser extent, managers may wonder about the suitability of their own positions for flexible work arrangements, about flexible work arrangements for staff they do not trust or whose evaluations are poor, about overhead (nonproductive time spent organizing flexible work training sessions or coordinating disparate schedules), or about the cost of the program. Misgivings about how to terminate flexible work arrangements and about the morale of nonparticipants are also common.

The answer to the control issue is twofold. First, managing by objective makes it possible to evaluate employees' work, regardless of any flexible work arrangements they may have. Second, effective communication and improved employee motivation resulting from flexible work increase job discipline. Still, the devil is in the details.

Interruptions In Supervision

All forms of flexible work limit the time and place of supervision. Differing shifts and/or locations of the employee and the supervisor separate them. This situation can either a problem or a benefit. A basic concept of flexible work is the transition from managing by monitoring to managing by objective [MBO]. In other words, an employee is not necessarily unsupervised because he or she is unobserved. Certainly, no worker is supervised just because a manager is nearby.

The way to supervise flexible workers and anyone else is to manage their work and monitor their results—rather than the other way around. Productivity, rather than procedure, is the main goal. Asynchronous management reduces the manager's obligation to watch constantly over workers, it relieves employees of the stress of observation, and it builds employee motivation. Objectives understood in common by management and employee effectively replaces line-of-sight supervision, a perfect solution to divergent hours and places of work.

Employee Abuse

Since flexible work arrangements are always subject to management approval, an employee who cannot responsibly handle flexible work is denied the opportunity to do poorly. Managers worry, however, about an employee cheating the employer of hours.

For example, a flextime worker might pretend to come in early, but actually arrive at a different time than agreed. To the extent that the output of an employee is well-defined, such deception cannot long stay concealed. As the number of flextime arrangements increase, the staff on the same alternative schedule will increase, and their presence will reduce idiosyncratic, deceptive behavior that might tempt a more solitary worker. Finally, some companies are introducing a modern variant of the time clock, a computer system that reads identification cards and tracks varying work schedules.

To account the time worked by telecommuters, most organizations use an honor system validated by measurement of employee productivity. That is, given the reported time worked, is the output commensurate? One of the reasons flextime reduces absenteeism is that workers repay its benefits with greater fidelity to the agreed flexible work schedules and, in the case of telecommuters, with longer hours worked per day.

Coordination and Availability of Telecommuters

Coordinating employees who come and go at different times is an important aspect of managing flexible workers. Some organizations allow employees to start the day only at certain times, or require that all employees must be present in the office at specified times or on particular days. Still others make team organization a priority; team leaders take responsibility for integrating work products of different staff. What flexible work inhibits is ad hoc approaches to intraorganizational coordination.

Certainly, the first principle of flexible work is that organizational requirements always take precedence. For those who must carefully coordinate their output or meetings with coworkers, their exercise of flexibility options must come second. Balancing workload, structuring schedule, and office presence are joint tasks of flexible workers, their co-workers, and management.

To the extent coordination is a problem for flexible workers, it is most often already a problem for everyone. Still, telecommuting and flextime make scheduling meetings, contacting employees who are off-site, and fostering team collaboration more time consuming. In organizations where the availability of staff is taken for granted, flexibility can frustrate those who rely on face-to-face interchanges.

A state of California telecommuter training session enumerated this frustration:

- Managers forget telecommuters' schedules and plan meetings during scheduled telecommute days
- Co-workers don't know when telecommuters will be in the office
- There is a sense that the telecommuter is never around
- There is a reluctance to call telecommuters at home
- Co-workers are not able to get in touch with a telecommuter
- Clerical staff are unclear on how or when to contact a telecommuter
- Telecommuters are reluctant to be away from the telephone, even to use the restroom.[18]

These problems can be solved by a regular telecommuting schedule known to co-workers, and by eliminating the taboo against calls to the home office.[19] On the other hand, a telecommuter should not be subject to random telephone inspection.

Flexible work arrangements can become more onerous as departments find themselves cutting back on clerical support positions or redirecting those positions to production; the hub role played by clerks, passing messages between professionals for example, improves coordination between telecommuters, flextime workers, and nontelecommuters. In a pilot, compressed work weeks and telecommuting resonated, creating some coverage problems on Fridays when most staff were absent. The conflict was resolved by alternating Mondays and Fridays for the alternate day off.

In offices with well-developed automation systems, computer-based schedulers, voice messaging, and electronic mail increase virtual presence. People are accessible and able to be scheduled independent of physical location. Many offices, of course, do not have these resources.

Telecommuting may reduce availability somewhat in organizations where schedules do not already face constant interference from field work, interdepartmental meetings, work-related travel, and authorized absences. Telecommuting can become a scapegoat for preexisting problems.[20] Organizations do not need to limit flexible work arrangements because of their impact on staff availability. However, they must commit to an increased level of intergroup planning, a point which must be emphasized in flexible work training and policy.

Flexible Work Burdens in Downsized Organizations

To understaffed organizations or to those facing severely imbalanced distributions of workload, flextime may seem a perfect way to make a bad situation worse. On the contrary, heavy workload and limited staff are appropriate conditions for flexible work because it reduces stress, and increases productivity with very modest expenditures. Managers must analyze workload, customer traffic, and other demands of the mission to be sure that all of the department's responsibilities are fully covered. They may be surprised to find that many employees will rally to longer work days when offered flexible work options.

Employee Resistance

Do workers resist telecommuting? There is little evidence that they do unless they are forced into full-time, home-based work in order to care for young children or to reduce their wages.[21] Predictions that the social isolation resulting from telecommuting leads telecommuters back to the office are uncorroborated.[22] For example, a program sponsored by the JC Penney Corporation in their telemarketing group (100 percent home-based, in fact) did not have a single "returnee" to the office among thirty-five workers in a two-year period.[23]

There may be resistance among workers who perceive that their career opportunities are diminished by telecommuting or among professionals who "need access to a relatively complex array of resources" that are not yet available electronically.[24]

Because working at home or on a flexed schedule is almost always voluntary for employees, those who don't wish to participate, don't. However, when a manager objects to flexible work, the option is foreclosed for all employees whether they would participate or not. Broad managerial support is a decisive element in the success—defined as participation and improved productivity—of flexible work initiatives.

Nonmanagement employees ususaly exercise flexible work options to the extent their work schedules and sites can be restructured. Fewer employees will choose home-based telecommuting than will choose flextime because of the costs and logistics of working from home. Still, in voluntary programs employee resistance is hard to measure. However, flexible work evlauations report that employees seldom choose to terminate telecommuting arrangements or flextime if not pressured by their supervisors to opt out. Indeed, most telecommuters increase their number of telecommute days if they can. Managers telecommute inconsistently because they fear that being away from their offices will compromise their roles.

Only when employees perceive a risk to their job status do they question participation. Employees may oppose telecommuting if flexible arrangements seem to threaten job security, create real or perceived barriers to job advancement, or increase costs of child care. Just as often, however, employees will forgo a promotion to retain or acquire flexible work options.

Although employees rarely forfeit their own flexible work options, those who do not elect to participate may go on to object to *other* flexible work arrangements in their work-group. Managers should watch out for complaints from nonparticipants that telecommuting is delaying their work or that flextime is unfairly increasing workload among those who work later in a shift. Legitimate issues of coordination and coverage need to be resolved, but rivalry for its own sake should be firmly and explicitly rebuffed by management.

Psychological Problems of Telecommuters

Psychological problems are widely promoted as drawbacks to telecommuting. Pop psychologizing typified by the remark of one business writer that "Psychological concerns are the overriding disadvantage of telecommuting," is rampant.[25] Isolation, loss of organizational identity, even workaholism are cited as threats to managers and employees alike. These concerns turn out to be largely speculative.

Telecommuter Isolation

According to Alvin Toffler, ". . . social isolation is the primary argument raised against work at home."[26] There are ample anecdotes which suggest that those who work at home *full-time* as independent contractors may experience social or professional isolation:

> "I have to have someone to talk to or to bounce ideas off of, or I go bananas," says an accountant who continues to work at home because it makes the most business sense.[27]

However, there is no factual data to support the generalization that those who telecommute part of the work week become isolated. On the contrary, some telecommuters experience a stronger sense of self-confidence and less dependence on co-workers than non-telecommuters.[28] The key seems to be whether telecommuters work full-time at home or come into work on a regular basis.

When telecommuters work *full-time* at home, they can feel cut off from informal communication among workers. One program lost a fifth of its sixty participants because returnees felt they were losing touch with the office grapevine as telecommuters.[29] A telecommuting program at the Federal Reserve Bank in Atlanta collapsed because of a communication gap between office-bound supervisors and telecommuters:

> "Basic but essential interchange between staff members and those they supervised really suffered," says Bobbie McCrackin, who telecommuted for the duration of the program, which lasted less than a year.[30]

Thus, it does not appear that working alone in and of itself is a problem for telecommuters, but if working away from the office becomes a barrier to communication, then the program can be jeopardized.

From an empirical perspective, it is unfortunate that many telecommuting studies examine full-time work-at-home arrangements. Their negative conclusions may be preordained by this focus. The Southern California Association of Governments (SCAG) telecommuting pilot did not find any problem with isolation among those who were away from the office only part of the work period.[31]

There are employees who meet their social needs at work. Toffler argues, however, that most people fulfill social needs through groups outside of work. The communication problems described above refer not to chit-chat around the water cooler, but to occupational isolation. This lacuna can be diminished by communications designed to maintain work-related exchanges among co-workers.

Studies of office computerization show that isolation is more a matter of work process than workplace. Automation may profoundly disturb workers in an office by eliminating collaboration and personal interaction. In one company, workers actually remained at work nearly an extra hour a day without pay to socialize with one another. Their company "went computer" and interpersonal interaction was replaced by solitary work in front of computer screens.

While effective communication between the office organization and the telecommuter is essential, there is no evidence that significant numbers of *part-time* telecommuters (full-time employees who telecommute only for a portion of their work period), longing for office society, will abandon remote work.

Organizational Loyalty

Reduced company loyalty, like isolation, is a telecommuting problem often predicted, but rarely observed. Instead of retaining employees, telecommuting is said to cause employees to become less loyal to their employers and more apt to jump ship than their office-bound colleagues. In its most dramatic form, the loss of loyalty is supposed to lead to *sunlighting*, the practice of working for other employers during one's telecommute day.[32] The futurist who first defined telecommuting, Jack Nilles, says flatly, "As people become successful in doing business from home, they often become consultants and go into business for themselves."[33] Certainly professionals become consultants, but there is no evidence that telecommuting encourages them to do so.

An Israeli transportation expert, Ilan Solomon, proposes that telecommuting, from an employer perspective, is self-negating:

 . . . The more off-site part-time employment succeeds, the more prone to failure it ultimately will become. The engagement of professional knowledge workers . . . is always a risky business. For the most part, their allegiances are more to their expertise and professional skills than to any employing organization. The remote, part-time employment arrangement further dilutes employer employee loyalty and commitment.[34]

Although Solomon sees flexible work as pouring gasoline on the fire, research demonstrates that autonomy on the job is loyalty-building, according to in-depth studies of employee satisfaction. Known internationally for her telecommuting studies, professor Patricia Mokhtarian of the University of California, Davis, suggests that while "the employee may respond to the company's open-mindedness and regard for worker morale with increased loyalty to the firm, [the] 'gratitude factor' is apt to fade . . . as telecommuting becomes more commonplace . . ."[35]

One careful study of organizational loyalty among telecommuters found that their affiliation quotient was statistically indistinguishable from nontelecommuting co-workers. Yes, professionals were found to be less loyal, but not because they were telecommuters. The differential in loyalty was a function of rank, with managers identifying significantly more with their employer than professional or technical employees.[36] In another study, telecommuting professionals showed greater loyalty to their work groups than to their company, but so did nontelecommuting professionals in the same organization.[37] Since we know that telecommuting programs often improve retention rates, however, loyalty can hardly be a casualty of flexible work. Telecommuting does not in itself appear to affect loyalty one way or another.

There is little doubt that the improved morale of telecommuters adequately offsets whatever organizational indifference flexible work engenders; as previously mentioned, flexible work may not always increase retention, but there is absolutely no evidence that it reduces loyalty.

Workaholism

Since professional and managerial workers routinely work uncompensated overtime at home, it is also possible that telecommuting increases the risk of overwork. The telecommuter, unlike the self-selecting supplementer, has probably established a more productive home work environment and may well have greater technological and information resources at hand. It therefore becomes easier and more productive for the telecommuter to work for longer periods and more intensively. According Margrethe Olson, head of the New York University Institute for the Study of Home-based Work, those tending to overwork may be at a disadvantage:

> The biggest problem [with telecommuting] is the tendency to work too much. . . . Electronic mail adds to this problem. The productivity benefits . . . go hand in hand with this downside because the machine itself and the accessibility it provides the at-home worker are compelling.[38]

Workaholism, like any behavioral addiction, can lead to stress-related illness, burnout, or family conflicts; these circumstances can rebound on the employer in lower productivity, sick leave, or interpersonal difficulties. Partly, workaholism is encouraged by professional and managerial status; these higher-paid, higher-status employees are urged by their positions neither to mind the clock nor work by it.

Olsen found that male telecommuters with limited social interests are the most likely to become workaholics.[39] If true, the trend to select telecommuters who are psychologically comfortable working alone may actually tend to encourage the workaholic to telecommute. If an organization sponsoring telecommuting has reservations about remote work, it may compensate by demanding of telecommuters a productivity windfall and reinforce tendencies to overwork.

However, the workaholic can feed his penchant at the office or the home. Indeed, the workaholic could be better off telecommuting because his excesses are less costly to a family, permit the integration of dinner breaks, and reduce the wear and tear of commuting.

Furthermore, workaholism (unlike alcoholism) doesn't necessarily lead to stress diseases or even unhappiness. Type A personalities, for example, are usually workaholic; until recently, it was assumed that they were more prone to heart attacks and other interruptions of lifestyle. However, the Framingham longitudinal study of heart disease showed that Type As may be more content and less subject to stress than Type B co-workers. Along the same lines, a study of thousands of randomly selected workers in Chicago showed that corporate executives were far happier with their workaholic lifestyles than clerical workers were with the nine-to-five containers in which they worked.[40]

Independent Contracting, a Slippery Slope

All employers, especially those with a hundred or more employees, use flexible workers to a significant degree. More workers work for temporary agencies than for any other kind of employer.[41] These are not regular, full-time employees who may work flexible hours or who may telecommute, but what the Conference Board calls contingent workers:

- part-time employees
- casual and seasonal workers
- contract workers
- retirees on service recall
- leased workers
- temporary workers

From an employer's perspective, contingent work is a cost-efficient solution to unusual workload. The hiring of a regular, full-time employee to solve short-term workload problems leads to overstaffing because when the workload peaks the increased staff becomes redundant. Contingent workers, such as consultants, may bring short-term expertise to an organization to solve nonrecurring, technical problems. These applications of contingent labor are not particularly controversial.

However, flexible work over the past twenty years has evolved to include the permanent use of contingent workers to replace positions formerly held by regular, full-time employees. In this instance, the employer gains at the expense of employees because the latter lose seniority rights and job security, fringe benefits, and possibly union representation typically available to regular, full-time staff. Savings on benefits (such as health care, sick and vacation leave, pension, disability, and unemployment insurance) can amount to 40 percent or more of a salary.[42] In an area where the labor pool is educated and experienced—as in a university community or high tech industrial region—an employer may also be able to avoid training costs by hiring skilled contingent workers even at a lower salary. A study of home-based computer professionals in

England found that their wages were 19 percent to 29 percent less than those performing comparable work in the office; the home-based workers also lost because they could not work overtime.[43]

There is no doubt that contingent employment has steadily become more popular with employers. From 1970 to 1986, employees working for temporary agencies grew from 184,000 to 760,000, an increase of 400 percent.[44] More than half of the net increase in U.S. jobs from 1980 to 1987 were among contingent workers; by 1987, almost a third of the American work force was contingent.[45] Today, 91 percent of all large companies are using contingent labor.[46] Some researchers believe contingent employment levels have crested. Others expect that companies will increase their use of contract workers by the end of the decade by at least one third and perhaps by as much as 100 percent compared to 1988.[47,48]

Downsized organizations may tacitly or explicitly encourage the use of contingent workers. For example, a fast-track budget approval procedure for contingent workers which at the same time places bureaucratically arduous (if not insurmountable) barriers to hiring permanent full-time staff quickly teaches a manager the corporation's flexible work policy. A company's chart of accounts may conveniently record expenditures for contingent workers in "non-people" categories such as overhead, contracting, or operations since it is their time or work products, not their labor, which is expensed. This keeps personnel dollars ostensibly lower and demonstrates—on paper at least—that a manager has ably controlled people costs or head count.

Employees, as well, may steer management towards contingent employment in proposals for job sharing, reduced hours, or variable hours.[49] In the University of California system (one of the largest employers in California), an employee can voluntarily waive health insurance benefits in trade for a shorter work week.[50] Not surprisingly, such a trade-off is usually oiled by a dual-income family in which a spouse, probably male, brings home a side of health insurance bacon.[51] In 1992, the Masco Corporation, the world's largest manufacturer of furniture, distributed a memo to its divisions explaining how to adjust part-time hours to minimize unemployment benefits if part-timers are laid off.[52]

There are evidently two kinds of flexible work, one referring to contingent employment, described above, and other referring to alternative work options such as flextime and flexiplace. The former becomes an issue for the latter in two ways.

First, in much of the literature of flexible work, the two are not clearly distinguished. This inspires a counter-reaction to flexible work by unions and others concerned that it degrades the workforce and threatens jobs. In several notorious telecommuting programs, companies used the term to ballyhoo the transformation of regular staff positions into independent contracts:

- A lawsuit by telecommuters against the Cal-Western Insurance Company is often cited; there, the company offered a "telecommuting" option to data entry clerks who were persuaded to forsake employee benefits in return, says the Insurer, "for the freedom to be their own employers, and to do their work at their leisure, when they wanted to do it."[53]
- In a Blue Cross "telecommuting" program, the telecommuters received about half the comparable salary and benefits of a regular employee performing the same work and were also charged by the insurer some $2,400 a year for computer equipment rentals.[54]
- In Los Angeles, a medical office leased employees whose pension benefits were less than those accrued in comparable employee positions.[55]

These problems can, to an extent, be defined away by categorically limiting flexible work options to full-time, career employees. However, skeptics will also worry about a slippery slope leading from flexible work to independent contracting. That is, a program begins honestly enough as a constructive alternative for employees, but ends up training managers to flex staff benefits, rights, and status. One workers' experience explains how this can happen, in the end returning her to her job but without benefits:

[Ms. Pat] Wingfield logged on to the trend [of telecommuting] by accident. She worked for BISYS' predecessor company for seven years and quit to move [90 miles] away. . . . The stay-at-home mom was starting to miss computer work when she breezed by the old office in December

1988 to show off her kids. When a former supervisor asked her to consult, Wingfield jumped at the chance. A month later she linked up with a computer, printer, phone, modem, and data line.[56]

The Association of Part-Time Professionals identifies job characteristics such as "project oriented positions . . ., creativity oriented positions . . ., [and] women in management. . . ." as lending themselves to reduced schedules.[57] These are the same job attributes usually identified with telecommutable positions. Opponents of flexible work may reasonably ask what safeguards are in place in a program to prevent managers from applying flexible work strategies in unintended ways?

To prevent the abuse of flexible workers, employers must have a clear policy that defines the responsibilities and the rights of telecommuters as full-time employees. Managers must be aware that their companies can be exposed to back pay fights and IRS fines if they cheat employees out of wages or benefits. Managers need to distinguish telecommuters from bona fide independent contractors.

Union Objections

It is prudent to consider, in general, trade union attitudes toward flexible work. By doing so, you increase the possibility of defining a program that won't unintentionally become encumbered with union opposition. In some organizations union perspectives on flexible work are unwelcomed. A union's voice, however, is recognized in many successful telecommuting programs. A thornier problem is that some employers as well as some unions oppose telecommuting proposals because of concerns with possible precedents. They see them as prima facie abridgements of prerogative. The program is said to risk the power granted by the collective bargaining agreement to one side or the other.

For example, although the county of Los Angeles reached accord with nineteen unions on telecommuting, it faced a grievance from a local Service Employees International Union (SEIU) bargaining unit. Management asserted that telecommuting is a management prerogative. The Local raised a raft of issues including check-off (union dues collected through the payroll system), workers' compensation, home costs, and promotional opportunities, especially for full-time telecommuters.[58] SEIU insisted "any issue is negotiable if it affects the wages, hours, and working conditions of a significant number of workers. . . ." Eventually, the county successfully negotiated flexible work issues with SEIU.[59]

The dispute with SEIU did not apparently prevent anyone eligible to telecommute from doing so, but there have been some effects of the dispute. "Eight hours agreements" detailing the start and end times of home-based clerical work are strictly enforced by management. Instead of signing a detailed telecommuter's agreement, telecommuters sign a statement acknowledging that telecommuting has been discussed with them.

In an especially nightmarish incident, a company and a union argued about whether a flexible schedule constitutes a shift. Shifts in this organization's union contract are awarded on the basis of seniority, but flextime schedules were established based on employee interests, job, and so forth. The union was also hostile to flextime schedules ending later in the day because they reduced the need for overtime from workers who normally left earlier.[60]

Certainly, the participation of unions adds to the planning overhead of a flexible work program. In some companies the union is not a player in telecommuting policy-making because union members are explicitly excluded from participation. This approach appears to insure less effective commute reduction, divides the workforce, denies flexible work options to those who may very much need them, and makes work policy mechanical rather than managerial.

Union objections have two foci: exploitation and organization. Instead of Toffler's electronic cottage liberating the work force, home offices were characterized as electronic sweatshops, where wages, hours, and safety are impossible to enforce.[61,62] The 1983 resolution of the AFL-CIO marked a decade of union opposition to telecommuting.

> [In this view] the home is . . . where women work in increasingly depersonalized jobs, in poor conditions, for menial, piece-rate wages and no benefits. Child exploitation is a possibility.[63]

Although this policy remains in effect, the AFL-CIO did adopt a resolution in 1991 that work at home by represented employees can be legitimate.

The practice of independent contracting described above has energized a broadside against telecommuting.[64,65] Work at home is a recipe for a "reserve army of the precariously employed," says Carla Lipsig-Mumme, a labor relations specialist at Quebec's Laval University.[66] "Home work in the 1800s," says John Zalusky, an AFL-CIO economist, "successfully competed with slave labor. At least the slave owner had to worry about caring for his property."[67]

True, geographical fragmentation may make it more difficult for unions to organize new members or to coordinate labor actions.[68] Union opposition to telecommuting is "quite understandable," says Elling. "A high degree of atomization of the labor force to homes or neighborhood centers can hardly be a dream situation for a union."[69] Unions can have a harder time communicating with telecommuting members through bulletin boards, getting them to meetings, or leafleting prospects.

There are several ways in which the union rights of the employee, and the organizational rights of the union can be acknowledged. The British trade union movement suggests that telecommuter computer equipment be used, among other ways, to foster communication between the employee and the union and with other employees. This is seen as a mechanism through which unions can service membership.[70] One employer gave the union space on a computer bulletin board created for telecommuters.

Unfortunately, some proponents of flexible work increase the opposition of organized labor by touting telecommuting and flexible work as anti-union alternatives. Part-time workers in one Wisconsin telecommuting project were limited to working weekly hours fifteen minutes under the minimum qualification for union membership.[71] The Association of Part-Time Professionals urges professionals go to nonunion companies for work, warning that a strong union at a company may inhibit managers from authorizing flexible work.[72]

A fundamental principle of flexible work is cooperation among interested parties, including unions. A constructive approach will probably pay off in a more successful flexible work program. In spite of the general opposition of the U.S. trade union movement to telecommuting, there are instances where unions and management have cooperated. The American Federation of State, County, and Municipal Employees (AFSCME) and the University of Wisconsin Hospital are working together in the program of telecommuting transcriptionists. A leader of the Local explained his organization's involvement: "We're seeing more people at remote work locations than we have in the past. To say it's not going to exist is not realistic. It's what our members want."[73]

The Hospital and the Wisconsin AFSCME Local have agreed to disagree on the selection criteria for telecommuters. The union only endorses telecommuter eligibility based on seniority, while the Hospital insists on a performance-based criteria for their selection. The issue has been moot because the most senior employees have also been those allowed to telecommute; newer employees work in the office until they acquire job experience.[74]

Promotional Barriers to Telecommuters

Telecommuters may worry that being out of sight will put them out of mind when management selects staff for promotions. Managers involved with Traveler Insurance Company's telecommuting program claim that "Your career may be plateaued while you're telecommuting." Explains Doug Willet, a second vice-president of human resources and data processing at the Travelers, "It's difficult to move up when you're not visible in the home office."[75] In other words, the telecommuter absents himself or herself from jockeying for position. Washington Post journalist Brian Starfire traces the scarcity of telecommuters to this precise issue:

> It would be nice if all managers managed by looking at your work product in a purely objective fashion. But in the real world, this doesn't happen. It's no secret that office politics plßay a big role in career development. And office politics doesn't travel well over a modem. . . .[76]

These assertions draw a reasonable distinction between the manager who merely supports the program and the manager who supports the program and its participants. In an office which runs on subjective judgments, it is possible a lukewarm sponsor of telecommuting may end up blaming participants for the option they've been encouraged to exercise.[77]

The absence of objective review of employee performance could, in certain scenarios, lead a telecommuter to argue that promotional opportunities were denied because of remote work. In organizations where performance counts most, telecommuters should be at less risk. This was Traveler's answer to calm fears among its telecommuters. Performance standards are set and applied even-handedly to telecommuters and nontelecommuters alike.[78] Still, telecommuters would be unwise not to put themselves forward, in person and regularly, to their supervisors and managers. Managers who consider office presence in promotional decisions should declare their criteria before a telecommuting program starts.

There will be workers who pass up promotional opportunities to retain positions that don't require full-time, on-site presence. An Apple Computer manager once requested (and received) a demotion in order to telecommute. Telecommuters and their managers must be clear with one another how permanent they expect a flexible work arrangement to be. Some flexibility consultants recommend a two-year limit on continuous telecommuting to avoid invisibility.[79] However, there is no way to arbitrate this issue by a rigid rule. The concrete circumstance of a position and the person who fills it have to be the bases of flexible arrangements and their longevity.

Flexible work works well when it is integrated into management's philosophy of operations. Otherwise, it can undermine employee relations. But what responsibilities do employees have in avoiding these problems? For one, remote workers need not be aloof workers. Telecommuters should to be active and visible participants in meetings, decision-making groups appropriate to their positions, and other work-related groups that engage the mission.

For another, the issues of promotion and new assignments should be explicitly raised by both management and employee. A flexible work policy should unambiguously exclude telecommuting and flextime from employee evaluation. Management avoids a double standard for telecommuters by evaluating not how work is done, but rather how well it is performed. For employees who create product—reports, technical analysis, computer programs—the plateau problem is minimized by these steps.

Supervisors and managers should take care to maintain an appropriate balance between their own needs for flexible work and their responsibilities to on-site employees. Where supervisors and managers have poor relations with subordinates, physical distance can symbolize managerial distance. Managers and supervisors should consult with their superiors about their own interest in telecommuting.

In general, managers and supervisors telecommute less frequently and more irregularly than the employees who report to them; however, their rates of participation may exceed those of other employee groups. They adjust their telecommuting schedule dynamically. Managers often telecommute for a few days to concentrate on writing a report. But when tensions rise during periods of heavy staff workload, supervisors should probably work on-site. Telecommuting by a supervisor at the expense of support for employees may be one instance where flexible work itself becomes a legitimate performance issue. Managers and supervisors often travel extensively because their jobs demand it. Whether time spent away makes it easier to telecommute (because managing at a distance is already understood), or more problematic (because hands-on management is already limited) is a question for highly mobile managers.

Inequity

In Japan telecommuting was for a time limited to a few top executives whose home-office suites were regularly cleaned by company janitors. However, what happens at the very top is somewhat removed from an organization's daily life; the highest level might be expected to march to the beat of its own drummer. What matters most are actions affecting the morale and commitment of managers and staff in the guts of an institution.

Among U.S. firms, elitism in flexible work takes on a possibly more pernicious form than in Japan. Inequitable opportunities to participate in flexible work options often highlight structural divisions with an organization's workforce. In some cases, telecommuting and flextime are limited to professional employees to whom a high degree of job autonomy is already granted.

Many organizations dabble in flexible work, and treat telecommuting and flextime as perks doled out to favored, most trusted staff. This approach is characterized by Kathleen Christensen, Director of the National Project on Home-Based Work at City University of New York: "Management can . . . use telecommuting as a lifestyle perk or in addition to a salary increase to entice high performers to stay with the firm."[80] The problem with managing flexibility as a perk for a chosen few is that bearing the load of a colleague working comfortably at home is enough to incite mob action.[77] Unless flexible work is a rationally distributed option, it is likely to cause resentment and rivalry within a work group. Managers who use telecommuting in recruitment must be especially wary of the feelings of those employees who haven't been offered flexible work arrangements.

In organizations that invite broader, more diversified participation, there can be severe differences between the way flexibility is implemented for professionals, for clerical workers, and for production workers. Sometimes, for example, telecommuting clerical workers will be intensively monitored by computer and telephone to see that they are home and how much they are working. The nature of many professional jobs prohibits such scrutiny. Thus, there may be increased autonomy for professionals and decreased autonomy for clerical workers.[82]

In some programs, clerical workers have been uncomfortable even taking a bathroom break lest their supervisors call when they are indisposed. One implementation required clerical telecommuters to call in before they could leave to pick their children up at school. There are supervisors so distrusting of flextime that they work twelve-hour days simply to supervise those coming in early or leaving late.[83]

One argument for combining flextime and telecommuting in a single program is that it broadens access to flexible work options from those whose particular jobs are readily telecommutable to employees who must work on-site. In fact, the Washington State Energy Office recommends that flextime options precede telecommuting to help acclimate an organization to flexibility. This excellent suggestion has the additional benefit of opening flexible arrangements to employees in more diverse positions.

At many companies, flexible work is a departmental-level prerogative with wide variations (even within a single department) in how it is handled. As an ironic rule, flextime and telecommuting in these instances are ruleless. Authorization is granted case-by-case, an approach that cuts two ways. So-called informal arrangements have the advantage of responding quickly to employee issues. However, because they are usually geared toward achievers, and lack formal procedures for resolving participation, ad hoc arrangements can invite gripe sessions by unhappy colleagues.[84] In larger organizations where managers are frequently transferred, informal arrangements can collapse as abruptly as summer camp romances; employees may have to constantly renegotiate their work lives.[85]

Companies are sometimes motivated to begin formal flexible work programs because they see a need to provide some direction, even regulation, to arrangements that have proceeded informally.[86] Managers can protect these arrangements (and themselves) by using a formal program to extend flexible work alternatives equitably. The best programs enable flexibility, formalize its policies and procedures, and aggressively promote participation without imposing it. They are rewarded with the largest gains in productivity, the lowest flexible work program costs per participant, and the least amount of controversy.

Conclusion

Despite its many benefits, flexible work remains a bold theory with great name recognition but limited practice. While the number of flexible work programs have expanded steadily over the years, the number of workers with alternative arrangements has grown only slightly.

The main reason for this paradox is management resistance and managerial fears of chaotic, uncontrolled work processes. They wonder about supervising people they can't see, and whether telecommuters and flextime workers won't cheat on their hours, effort, or results. Flexible work arrangements can actually enhance management's hand by the systematic application of management by objective.

Managers also are concerned about employee availability, as well as maintaining cooperation and teamwork among flexible workers and traditional workers. Part-time telecommuting, good office organization, and thoughtful scheduling will make the telecommuter and flextime worker adequately available and able to work well with colleagues.

Despite a lot of speculation, part-time telecommuters do not suffer from social or occupational isolation, although there is some risk of isolation among full-time telecommuters. Telecommuters do not put one foot out the door by telecommuting; they are as loyal if not more loyal than nontelecommuters.

Unfortunately, problems associated with independent contracting and the contingent workforce have become confused with flexible work. By keeping these practices clearly distinguished, the biggest risks to flexible work are avoidable. Unions have seen the consequences of independent contracting in terms of their interests, and defining a company flexible work program clearly is an important step to working with rather than against organized labor.

Telecommuters may have some problems maintaining their visibility in an office, especially when promotions are being considered. They must use their on-site time to compensate.

The opportunity to participate in flexible work may be inequitably distributed between groups of employees, among types of positions, and even between two people in a division. While these inequities are not characteristic of flexibility, they must be consciously avoided.

6

The Selection and Management of Flexible Workers

You've put together a wonderful flexible work program. Your goal is to support your business and your people. You've sculpted traditional and innovative personnel policies until they meld like hand and glove. The CEO issued a mandate for flexible work as inspired as the Declaration of Independence, as down-to-earth as a balance sheet. Training plans have jelled. Employees count their new options, managers and supervisors look forward to taking on change. Press releases are ready to fax about the company's enterprising steps to support the family and reduce commuter glut.

Unfortunately, many flexible work programs then trip on their own shoelaces when it comes time to select telecommuters and flextime workers. Selection turns planning into practice, goals into results—and, too often, expectations into disappointments. Organizational and employee benefits of flexible work are proportional to the breadth and depth of the selection process. Which employees are eligible to participate? How many of them actually do? Is the program for a few or for many? Will it favor professionals and ignore clerks and technicians—or just the reverse? What seniority level, performance record, or commuting distance from home qualify telecommuters?

Suppose, for example, a company would like to increase productivity, enhance air quality, and improve morale. These are excellent grounds for establishing telecommuting and flextime programs. To estimate the potential return on effort, a management analyst might divide the workforce into three groups based on an understanding of the kind of work performed: those who could regularly telecommute or flex their time (every week), those who could occasionally (a few days each month), and those who cannot flex work arrangements at all.[1]

However, the group to which an employee is assigned is not inevitable. A selection *philosophy* posts them one way or another. Management decides what work is appropriate for flextime or telecommuting, which employees are appropriate, which of their supervisors are appropriate, and even at the eleventh hour, if the program is still appropriate.[2] Because the selection process determines the scope of participation in a flexible work program, no other facet of flexibility brings forth as much advice, including bad advice, from the popular press, company pundits, and consultants. And since selection all by itself can determine whether a program is well done or undone, managers need to be especially clear about how they will handle it.

The bottom line of the selection process is gatekeeping. Despite an exploding rise in employee interest in telecommuting, the flexiplace and telecommuting arrangements begun in nearly all organizations have admitted only an elite few.[3] The selection methods many programs use assure minimal participation. Often, flexible work has so many preconditions for participation that few employees qualify. These preconditions may reflect piloting objectives, fears of loss of managerial control if the numbers of participants grow large, or the assumption that most employees cannot be trusted with work without constant monitoring.

Perhaps the greatest challenge facing flexible work is whether or not it can become a large-scale program to improve the quality of work life, the quality of personal life, and productivity.[4] It's easily demonstrated that flexible work programs have little impact on commuting unless they have broad participation. Other individual benefits of flexible work become unimpressive if they are accrued by only a fraction of an employer's workforce. Among the issues identified in flexible work, level of participation controls the extent of transportation demand management, productivity, employee satisfaction, and the benefits of management-by-objective.

There are four major selection issues to consider: (1) To what extent should employee personality determine suitability for telecommuting and flextime? (2) In what ways does an employee's job description and work history determine telecommutability? (3) If and how are professionals selected? (4) If and how are clerical and technical employees selected?

In practical terms, these issues are much simpler for flextime programs than for telecommuting programs. Traditional supervision and worksites are only slightly modified by flextime arrangements; employees still come to work and remain physically accessible to supervisors and co-workers for most of the workday. Coverage of work assignments, coordination among partners in a production process, employee security arrangements and access to facilities during off-shift periods, and collective bargaining agreements set the limits of the flextime option.

Within these limits, thousands of companies use voluntary flextime easily and successfully. Where individual problems arise they are addressed individually. At least one company in the United States—the Joy Cone Company in Hermitage, Pennsylvania, a manufacturer of ice cream cones—and a department store in Germany have organized flextime programs entirely based on self-selection; workers propose their schedules each month (except for seasonal periods of peak demand), which are then arbitrated to assure coverage.[5] These programs have worked well for many years, and boast high productivity and low turnover. Throughout the United States, nurses in many hospitals elect their own shifts. About 60 percent of all cancer nurses in outpatient facilities, for example, have autonomy in setting starting and ending times at the beginning of their employ.[6] Subsequent changes are approved so long as adequate nursing coverage is provided. This option is a well-established carrot to a labor group traditionally in short supply. Now that the supply of nurses is beginning to exceed demand for them, perhaps that inducement will be curtailed. The selection of telecommuters, however, is another story.

The Telecommuter Personality

Among the factors of successful telecommuting touted loudly by many practitioners and most of the press are choosing the right people to telecommute and the right people to manage them. For example, a Pacific Bell manager—whose company aggressively markets telecommuting to business customers—advises that "what counts in telecommuting has more to do with the person than the tasks."[7] Consultants or flexible work program managers may base selection on psychological questionnaires, written self-assessments, and most recently, interactive computer programs designed to appraise an individual's personal suitability for telecommuting. Indeed, considerations of other program components, notably technology and training, pale in comparison with the emphasis on personnel factors found in management periodicals, computer publications, and the spate of success magazines published for professionals, working women, and entrepreneurs. The emphasis on choosing the right people, of making highly individualized assessments of an employee's suitability, and the belief that only those with special personal qualities can dance the dance has one certain outcome: few employees will participate, and of those that do, nearly all will be highly paid professionals.

Not only is there probably undue concern about selecting the right people, but frequently the personal selection criteria are unreasonable. For instance, a telecommuting consultant suggests profiling an employee to exhibit the telecommutable aspects of a job, the fit of the employee's personality to telecommuting, and the relationship of the employee to his or her manager. "If [the relationship] is not good, you're starting out on the wrong foot . . . Telecommuting is based on mutual trust."[8] Some even advise a review of a telecommuting arrangement if the job's, supervisor's, or employee's motivation or ability to work independently change.[9]

If trust is based on an employee's work history, it has some factual basis. However, trust deriving from a good working relationship may be lacking where two people dislike one another and prefer to relate as little as possible. Such circumstances arise all the time in organizations. If this lack of rapport ends up barring flexible work options for an employee, antagonisms may only intensify and legitimate equity concerns could be raised.

Other consultants and managers have other guidelines for selecting ideal candidates for flexible work as these comments show:

"You must have people with a high degree of integrity," says Jack Daley, manager of corporate telecommunications for Tymshare.[10]

"A telecommuter should be self-motivated, self-disciplined, and work well independently. If a person has a low need for social interaction he's more likely to adjust to the home setting."[11]

"While the type of job must translate well to a home environment, so too must the personality of the employee. A telecommuter must be capable of handling autonomy."[12]

"[In published] interviews with management and employees at various companies with telecommuting experiments . . . a common theme expressed was carefully choosing persons to work from home . . . Almost a quarter of the articles recommended only highly motivated employees work from home."[13]

What is troubling about these assertions is that they offer no data to prove that these qualities play an essential role or that, in their absence, telecommuters perform poorly, give up remote work, or are asked by managers to return to the office. Furthermore, many clerical telecommuting positions not only do not require autonomy, they make no room for it.

One psychological study of telecommuters found that they were not any more autonomous, no more focused on personal organization, and no less social than nontelecommuters.[14] That is, all of the requisite attributes of a successful telecommuter were wanting; they did exhibit a greater desire to understand their work than nontelecommuters. Interestingly, telecommuters in the study were also more affiliated, that is, more loyal to their employer than nontelecommuters—exactly the opposite of what many pop psychologies of telecommuting assert.

Telecommuting is not a solo sail around the world where, presumably, months of isolation and stormy seas take a certain disposition to handle. Part-time telecommuting, especially, is rather like going away to a conference, yet no one has their personality assessed before being asked to travel. Indeed, on-the-job travel is always viewed as a job requirement, its familiar strains notwithstanding. Similarly, outside sales forces have always been evaluated according to their sales productivities, not their personal proclivities.

Here lies an irony of managerial culture. Telecommuting, with its palpable reductions in stress and boons to productivity, sets some managers searching for the right kind of people. However, extensive and stressful out-of-town assignments sets them searching for the right kind of airfare. If telecommuting was viewed routinely, like travel or outside sales, telecommuters would be selected routinely; the irony would iron itself out.

The first few times working at home, telecommuters are likely to have problems such as forgotten documents or a missing copy of the company telephone directory. These oversights don't reoccur often; when a telecommuter is stuck at home, without the proper materials and unable to work, once burned is twice learned. The lesson comes with experience rather than with a personality *predisposed* to successful telecommuting.

Those who insist on a telecommuter persona conjoin the idea that managers of telecommuters also need an appropriate persona. Futurist Jack Nilles says "what we try to find out is whether the manager is comfortable with the idea of telecommuting."[15] His consulting firm, JALA Associates, identifies the following managerial qualities as factors in a successful telecommuting program:

1. Focus on work activity for evaluation
2. Focus on work product for evaluation
3. Effective communication with staff
4. Priority of communication with staff
5. Level of trust from and with staff
6. Quality of innovation, flexibility
7. Quality of structure, "playing by the rules"[16]

Yet on the contrary, in a psychological study of telecommuting, no statistical link could be found between managerial style and managerial comfort with telecommuting; both task-oriented and person-oriented managers were equally content managing telecommuters.[17] The ability to manage a remote worker comfortably was unrelated to differences in managerial personality.

Moreover, which of those managerial skills are ever superfluous? Telecommuting is besides the point in this list of basics. Good management always implies effective communication, focus on activity and products, trusting staff relations, innovation, and fair play. One argument for telecommuting is that it strengthens management in just these ways.

Selection based on personality is a theorem without a proof. Futhermore, it can trespass on employee privacy. It is one matter for a telecommuter to bring work home and blur the distinctions between work and nonwork. It is quite another for *management* to render social and psychological judgments about an employee's home environment.

For example, one commentary on telecommuting advises against telecommuting by employees with a history of conflict at home.[18] How would a manager know about home conflicts, and if he did, is it appropriate for management to act on such information? This spurious logic ignores the fact that many conflicts at home trace back to schedule problems caused by work! Telecommuting might therefore reduce conflicts at home rather than be burdened by them. Some selection processes ask employees to reveal information about their personal lives which verge on intrusion. One program asked its employees to explain "why do you want to stay at home to work? . . . How does telecommuting fit into your home environment? By working at home, can you work more hours? . . ."[19] It is a short distance from questions like those to paternalistic decisions. A telecommuter orientation package states, for example:

> We also wish to avoid situations where home telecommuting may aggravate family tensions. In short, we wish to avoid placing people in situations where we feel that telecommuting may not be a good idea for them.[20]

While there are people who wouldn't be comfortable working at home for any number of reasons (one article calls poor candidates for telecommuting "'social' persons . . . for whom the stimulation of the office environment is one of the main pleasures of going to work . . ."), they need not volunteer.[21] Management, however, has no rational basis for selecting out such people and disapproving telecommuting "for their own good."

Managers, like anyone exercising authority over others, make their own estimates of the dispositions, feelings, and attitudes of the people they manage. Wise managers keep these estimates to themselves or at least in high confidence. No one would tolerate a manager's psychological assessment in an annual performance evaluation except in extraordinary circumstances (national security positions or possibly law enforcement). Even if such approaches were demonstrably helpful in the selection of telecommuters, their precedent would be so odious as to be unacceptable. Indeed, psychological assessments are exceedingly difficult even when attempted by experienced, licensed professionals. Witness the contradictory opinions that flood a courtroom when psychologists take the stand. The manager need not don the therapist's hat; his own should be big enough to handle the selection of flexible workers.

Does this suggest that managers retreat from responding to employee needs for flexible work? Not at all. Rather, the family friendly manager places the initiative with employees by soliciting volunteers. Telecommuters should be advised in training sessions about potential conflicts working at home can generate and how to cure them. However, the specifics are for the employee to consider, not for management to assess or adjudicate.

Telecommutability

The recommended alternative to selection based on personality is selection based on the telecommutability of a job: the extent to which the tasks required of it are independent of the location of the worker. Among the tasks that characterize a job, some or all may be location-independent.[22] This perspective, for example, makes part-time telecommuting feasible since one can shoulder parts of a job at a remote location.

The notion of breaking down a job into discrete components has its roots in so-called principles of scientific management first enumerated by Frederick Taylor in the 1930s and is still popular today. Jobs would be designed by figuring out the most efficient way to carry out each task and then assembling the tasks into a whole. The famous time and motion study reflects the idea that a job can be studied—and perfected—separately from the person performing it.

With the advent of automation, computerized industrial process control, and a better educated workforce, motivational theorists put the worker back into the work by advocating increased employee discretion, teamwork, and the elimination of piece-rates in many industries.[23] Nowadays, scientific management is a mélange of theories. One finds holistic philosophies of worker motivation implemented side-by-side with retrofitted piece-rating (as in computerized counts of keystrokes/hour or other time and motion measures of productivity). Similarly, management-by-objective sometimes provides workers opportunities to exercise independence and self-direction in processing their work, while sometimes it conceals a traditional focus on supervisory control and task-minding.

Telecommuting was born into this conglomeration of management ideologies. Telecommuting theory is a composite with varying stresses: Tayloristic deconstructions of work, psychologies of the autonomous worker, even sociologies of the remote worksite. However, the simplest and least jargon-strewn theory of telecommuter selection is telecommutability.

The telecommutability of a job is analyzed by asking a series of factual, practical questions about the nature of its duties.[24] These questions can be distributed to interested employees as guidelines for the telecommuter applications described in the previous chapter. Although this format, as a whole, is oriented toward professional positions, individual questions also pertain to field assignments (such as sales and inspection positions), technical positions (such as detectives and computer operators), and clerical employees (such as data-entry clerks and customer service representatives in telemarketing firms).

Telecommutability Analysis

Personal contact

1. What percentage of the job is devoted to face-to-face contact with other agencies or departments, the public or internal staff?
2. Can this contact be revamped to allow for communications via telephone or can such contact be limited to nontelecommuting days?
3. Are parts of the job sufficiently self-contained so that they can be performed independently of co-workers, and, if necessary, integrated into the whole later?

Concentration

1. How fragmented is work by short-notice, short turnaround assignments?
2. How fragmented is work into tasks requiring high concentration?

Project orientation

1. Can tasks that can be completed at home be grouped and scheduled for telecommuting days?

2. Are job activities project-oriented so that tasks are structured flows of information (such as reports) due in a defined time frame?
3. Are there defined milestones or deliverables at specified times?

Required Access to Resources

1. Does the telecommuter have all the knowledge needed to work at home, or will she or he need supervision or input from others that is only available on-site?
2. Is physical access to special resources necessary?
3. What percent of the job uses resources only available on-site?
4. Can these resources easily be taken home for a day or two?
5. Can access needs be grouped for nontelecommuting days?
6. Is much need for working space associated with the job?

Activities

1. Can the paperwork of the job be done at home?
2. Does the job involve routine information handling?

Travel

1. Can trips begin or end at home rather than the office?
2. Does the job involve field work?

Security

1. Does job-related information require physical security?
2. Does the job sensitive information that can be protected by means other than physical security (such as encryption)?

Technology

1. Are there special equipment requirements such as high-quality printers, high-speed modems, photocopiers, or facsimile capability?
2. Is there a need for complex equipment support?
3. Is there a high use of the telephone?
4. Are terminals or computers necessary for the job, or can one be used to accomplish a large part of the work?

None of these questions have right answers. Most positions are partly portable, partly facility-bound. With these characteristics, a reality check on which activities dominate day-to-day work, and common sense, it is straightforward to identify which jobs are suited to part-time, occasional, or majority-time telecommuting—and which are completely unsuited. By answering these questions, employees can dependably assess their own telecommuting potential.

Screening Telecommuters' Applications

Suppose that a pool of interested employees have completed their applications; they have convincingly appraised what work they could do at home and proposed a schedule for doing so. What next? This phase of selection brings management to screening the applicants' personnel folders.

Screening is fairly objective. The most often-consulted fact is job experience within the organization, which is measured by both seniority (length of service) and positions held. (Below the relevance of job experience acquired in other organizations is considered.) The JC Penney Company requires a year of in-office experience, for example, before it allows its telemarketers to work from home.[25] Consultant Gil Gordon recommends at least six months of seniority, while some consider as little as three months acceptable provided the employee understands fully his or her agency's operation.[26,27]

The problem with a rigid seniority requirement is that it obviates the recruitment benefits telecommuting can bring. A top candidate for a position whose job offer includes telecommuting would probably not accept a waiting period of up to a year. Some individuals may have a good understanding of an organization gained through other means than formal job experience; one university telecommuter, for example, did extensive work with her future employer while attending graduate school.

It does make sense that an employee who has little idea how an organization works, is on probation, and is not known by co-workers will want to break in the new job before spending much time away from the office. The point is that there will be exceptions in a thoughtful program.

The second most commonly advocated screening criteria is performance record. Here, Gordon recommends a score of at least three on a five-point scale:

Here is somebody who knows the job well enough and whose performance is solid enough to earn [a manager's] trust. We want somebody who's been on the job long enough to answer many of their own questions and solve many of their own problems.[28]

Intuitively, an employee with a history of poor performance needs more supervision, not less; telecommuting would seem to send the problem in the wrong direction. Again, however, there can be exceptions. Sometimes poor performance is tied to personal situations which are resolved by flexing time and/or place of work. Many workers will not reveal negative personal circumstances or would feel guilty about using them to explain job problems.

However, some proponents recommend that only high achievers telecommute.[29] This approach renders telecommuting a de facto reward; it is not a programmatic approach but a way to make a deal. Sometimes conflicts with a supervisor get in the way of high ratings and create morale problems that could actually be reduced by telecommuting. Consequently, even poor performance history may not automatically disqualify a potential telecommuter. It would, however, raise flags. Management might take a chance, and offer a limited telecommuting trial with clear direction to the employee that unless performance improves, telecommuting cannot continue.

Avoid Catch-22 syndromes. An employee was habitually late to work; when flextime was introduced, he was excluded from participating on the basis of his performance record. The reason he was late was because he, not his wife, had to bring their children to daycare, while she could pick them up afternoons. The supervisor, unable to see his employee's family responsibilities as they were, never understood how flextime would be a win-win for employee and employer. And he didn't want to coordinate different start times. So, they spent time each week arguing about time rather than doing something about it.

Stereotyping the Flexible Worker

Even supposedly objective programs, with their focus on job duties to assess telecommutability, often fall victim to stereotypes of the workforce that limit action. Some, as discussed earlier, are gender-based and out of step with the dual income family and the single head of household commonly found in the workforce today. Others, perhaps more pervasively, favor professionals over clerks.

Attitudes toward professional work and clerical work are deeply seated in our culture and language. Consider how one thesaurus associates other roles with these highly suggestive terms:[30]

Professional	*Clerk*
Adviser	Bureaucrat
Artist	Civil Servant
Authority	Official
Expert	Pen-pusher
Guru	Scribe
Master	Secretary
Official	Salesperson
Specialist	Shopkeeper
Veteran	Vendor

They only share the "Official" role, which can mean the low status of a receptionist or the high status of an elected official. In concept, the professional brings employers value, experience, and knowledge while the clerk brings mere labor. Professionals are "workers doing cognitive tasks that require specialized knowledge gained through lengthy education, with a graduate degree, or through special certification or licensing."[31] Not surprisingly, these sharp contrasts strongly influence flexible work programs.

Settled professionals, the bright collar workers, are omnipresent in the media as baby boomers with babies who are unwilling to have their lives controlled by the organizations that employ them.[32,33] At the same time, their work is somewhat understood to "oscillate between needing solitary concentration and active collaboration . . . with others across skill and functional boundaries."[34] Their activities as workers—reading, writing, travel, informal meetings in person or on the telephone—are readily characterized as location independent.[35] Many of these professional activities, of course, are routinely performed off-site as uncompensated overtime. Nowadays, hotels advertise modem-ready telephones, desk space, and other accoutrements of the home office so the traveler can work at night. Thus, when a company does allow telecommuting, the professional worker is a far more obvious candidate for working at home than the clerical worker.

There are subtle ways in which a professional staff may compete with a clerical staff for telecommuting slots. While the private secretary has all but vanished from the corporate landscape, the support functions she once accorded are still commonly provided, only now by clerical pools: telephone reception and screening, word processing, document management (filing, duplication, distribution), purchasing, travel and meeting arrangements, and so forth.

When the professional telecommutes, these functions conveniently link the home office to the office organization. The clerical pool can evaluate whether a telephone call should be transferred to the telecommuter, distribute a memo faxed into the office, or otherwise coordinate on-site and off-site communication. These functions update the traditional support provided a traveling professional. Despite technologies that can substitute for clerical support, managers may feel an office will become unglued if both clerks and professionals are working from home; with clerks absent, who will coordinate the professionals? Telecommuting becomes an either/or concept.

In one systematic survey of executives more than half thought professionals could telecommute, more than half thought clerical workers could telecommute. However, those in the former group tended not to be in the latter. Most managers saw telecommuting potential for professional staff *or* for clerical staff, but *not* for both. Of those who stated clerical workers could telecommute, most saw telecommuting as a program for parents, particularly mothers with young children.[36] Thus, there can be both value, labor, and gender judgments in comparisons of the professional to the clerk.

The attitude toward clerical telecommuting in the literature is often negative. For example, computer writer John Seymour dismisses clerical telecommuters:

> As workers learn that they can reach colleagues in other satellite offices as easily by computer as they once did by walking down the hall—and can exchange documents, budgets, schedules, and plans through high-speed modems while discussing revisions on a second telephone line—they fall hard for the idea of suburban offices. This scenario is a giant

step beyond the obsolete, limited vision of clerical telecommuters handling repetitive data-entry from their dining tables. As with other innovations, the idea didn't have much appeal to management until more valuable processes were involved.[37]

It would not appear that clerical workers are expected to exchange documents and the like, although any successfully automated organization would soon find its document production constipated if clerks were not in the electronic loop. What's at work here is a presumption that the new technologies and new ways to work both became valuable when professionals started using them, and so clerical workers, like the work they do, are not valuable.

Similarly, the well-regarded Israeli sociologists, the Solomons, presume that clerical workers cannot accept the lifestyle changes flexible work engenders:

> Changes in lifestyle, as defined by Solomon, are major life decisions that are deeper in their nature than a simple change in work location. This leads us to develop the hypothesis that only a limited degree of acceptance [of flexible work] can be expected from the larger groups of white-collar employees, namely those who hold rather routinized clerical jobs.[38]

Why clerical workers would be less able to engage in major life decisions than their professional co-workers is never explained. In one telecommuting program, clerical workers were randomly telephoned several times a day to make sure they were working, while professional workers were not. This program also required clerical workers to telephone their supervisor for permission to leave their home cum office to run an errand, while professionals managed their time without seeking approval for a brief interruption of work.

Participation of clerical workers in flexible work programs raises several issues:

- The majority of clerical workers are women; thus, debates over options for flextime and telecommuting often surfaces a debate over telecommuting as a solution to domestic care.
- The debate over independent contracting is more intense with respect to clerical telecommuters than professional workers because the degree of recorded abuse is far greater.

- Unions in organizations sponsoring flexible work often represent clerical workers, especially in governmental organizations; hence, union perspectives on flexible work can modulate clerical participation rather more than professional participation.

There appear to be blocks to significant clerical participation in many telecommuting programs. For example, a progress report of the state of California telecommuting pilot noted during the middle of the project that:

> At least half of California's 140,000 state employees are information workers. They are people who analyze or manipulate data, and they have the potential to telecommute. . . . Which jobs are ripe for telecommuting? In our pilot program they range from clerks and transcriptionists doing word processing to program analysts, contract reviewers . . . [and other professionals].[39]

No distinction is drawn between the suitability of clerical workers and of professionals for telecommuting. However, when the final report was issued, the participation rate of professionals and managers was *20 times* greater than the clerical participation rate.[40] In Los Angeles County exciting benefits were realized by clerical telecommuting. One group of data-entry clerks consistently doubled their daily productivity and halved their error rate when they worked at home. Furthermore, clerical participation was guaranteed by the county's telecommuting policy. Nonetheless, their participation rate (measured against the total number of clerical workers) was *half* that of professionals and managers.[41]

In one study of management attitudes towards telecommuting, managers said motivation was a key qualification of professional telecommuters, but not of clerical telecommuting. Clerical output of clerks was "routine [and] repetitive" and therefore easily regulated.[42] The study found that clerical telecommuting was typically associated with reducing labor costs (by pushing clerical work out the door to home-based contract labor), while professional telecommuting was authorized to increase the freedom to concentrate and be creative. The authors concluded that "When telecommuting is adopted . . . the organization of telecommuting programs tend to exacerbate current inequalities in workplace."[43]

Historian of work Monica Elling seconds this sentiment, explaining that:

> There exists a risk of the development of a polarization between different occupational groups. Well educated 'professional' workers can improve their situation under conditions in which remote work provides maximum flexibility. They can, for example, commute between the home workplace and the 'real' workplace without risk of a deterioration in working conditions. On the other hand, employees performing routine work tasks with low educational requirements can risk becoming trapped in isolated home work with piecework wage forms.[44]

Computerization, whether on-site or remote, may contain the seeds of polarization. "It is speculated that the increased flexibility might accrue to the executive and professional occupations, with increased rigidity perhaps characterizing the clerical occupations."[45] Modern office automation makes it easy to count keystrokes or other piecework measures of productivity whether or not an hourly rate is paid. However, flexible work does not *cause* polarization even though it will reflect *existing* polarization.

Arguably, a clerical worker with children may need flexible work even more than a professional with children because the former's lower income draws on fewer options for home care and child care, an elusive resource for any parent. For example, clerical workers rely more on low-paid or unpaid child care by neighbors, relatives, and friends than do professionals.[46] Professionals, on the contrary, use institutionalized day care. In-home care may be less yielding to work schedules (because its givers are themselves encumbered with their own work and child-care responsibilities), and thereby increase the need for flexible scheduling.

A flexible work program will need to take emphatic actions— with specific, numerical goals—if it intends clerical workers to participate to any significant degree.

Technical and field workers fall into a gray zone, and share stereotypes with both clerical workers (whose output is emphasized) and professional workers (whose input is emphasized). Examples of technical workers include police and probation officers, inspectors of all kinds, computer and telecommunication system operators, or graphic artists, draftsmen and draftswomen.

Like clerical workers, the telecommuting potential of technical workers is usually less than obvious to managers and supervisors. In fact, their jobs may be just as portable as a professional's. Detectives, for example, may spend 40 percent of the work week on paperwork they could do in a home office; in Palo Alto, California, and Los Angeles, detectives regularly telecommute. Remote management of computer systems—such as telephone central office equipment—allows technicians to work from home rather easily. The continuing depression of computer pricing, matched by a continuing increase in power, allows telecommuters to work on all kinds of graphic productions (blueprints, industrial design, book jackets).

Field workers, including outside sales forces, inspectors, assayers, meter readers, to name but a few, are also excellent candidates for telecommuting. Federal agencies routinely establish home as the headquarters of field workers (such as inspectors for regulatory compliance); they report to offices only for meetings (by the way, these workers are not considered telecommuters since their homes are their official duty stations). A number of computer and telecommunication companies have dispersed their sales forces to their homes.

As more objective criteria for selecting flexible workers takes hold, a much broader group of positions exhibit telecommuting potential. The successful selection process unlocks latent benefits in productivity, morale, and retention by putting the job, not the job holder, on center stage; other, more personally oriented criteria should only then come into play. This two-stage approach to selection fully releases the positive energy of a flexible work program.

The Challenge of Managing Flexible Workers

For workers to change the ways they work, managers will need to change the way they manage. Companies are organizational structures that encourage personal contact whether it helps get work done or not.[47] Those managers who are accustomed to receiving oral input from others on the fly have a hard time with remote work.[48] To become self-confident supervisors of off-site work, managers need to overcome the attitude that their effectiveness depends on monitoring employee work and managing face-to-face.[49]

Managers need to see a new way to relate to their employees.[50] Flexible work requires management flexibility, a stance emphasizing employee products rather than observations of work processes and more conscious, structured communication with employees. Managers accustomed to traditional supervision must experience a shift in thinking before they can embrace flexible work. These changes are fundamental to the viability of all formal flexible work programs.

Part of the problem is that managers do not readily identify with prospective flexible work arrangements, and it is therefore harder for them to see another point of view. Executives polled about flexible work usually describe it as a work option for others, not for themselves.[51] Ironically, once a program gets underway managers telecommute frequently. For example, in one study of a flexible work program, managers *expected* their rate of telecommuting to be distinctly less than nonsupervising staff, while their *actual* participation rate was higher once the program began.[52] Presently, some 5 percent of Pacific Bell's managers telecommute, making them the single largest group of telecommuters in the company.[53] Among 700 telecommuters in Los Angeles County government, 20 percent are managers.[54] When managers personally experience telecommuting, their attitudes toward it change. Some managers may need to see firsthand how well it works before they can support a flexible work program for their employees.

Office Communications in a Flexible Work Program

In managing successful flexible work arrangements, the biggest problem to solve is communication between co-workers (including their managers). For example, flextime requires that workers find ways to pass information to one another that do not depend on being in the same place at the same time. Communication with flexiplace workers, similarly, requires spanning the distance that now separates them. Telecommuters, separated by both time and place, need communication links that bridge both.

Communication is a challenge because flexible work disrupts the trusted communication channels of an office. Indeed, the office can be viewed as a highly efficient communication network, where physical closeness advances collaboration among employees. Communication is formatted by people working in the same area, sharing an office, hallway, or entire building.[55] The *Personnel Journal's* Carol-Ann Hamilton observes that proximity tolerates sketchy communication:

> You develop some bad habits when your staff is clustered about you. You don't have to be as concise or consistent in the way you inform because workers who don't understand a task can yell across the hall, "Hey, what's this all about?"[56]

The informality and spontaneity of face-to-face communications at the workplace helps a manager to manage the proverbial crisis, when the novel, ambiguous, or unexpected suddenly threatens the day-to-day order of the organization.[57] But we are well into the second hundred years of the information society, a 9-1-1 community in which picking up the telephone is not merely practical, it is the preferred response to predicament. When crisis hits, telecommunications quickly unites the organizational forces needed to restore harmony. Physical proximity is a management convenience, not a daily necessity. Managers know how to manage a crisis with the telephone—they do it all the time.

During workaday conditions, management by objective is the method for achieving concise and consistent communications between management and staff. Many informal conversations at the worksite are catch-up solutions to confusion spawned by poorly delivered information, imprecise direction, misunderstandings over assignments, or just vague, slatternly communication. How many informal meetings, in other words, are attempts to understand what other meetings really meant? Management by objective reduces the need for informal communications, while telecommunications and on-site days allow extemporaneous exchanges with remote workers when circumstances require it.

Only full-time telecommuting lodges any risk of so severely disrupting informal communication channels that the worker becomes organizationally disassociated. This risk is yet another reason why full-time telecommuting is best left as a solution to highly unusual situations. For the most part, communications will thrive in a mix of office hours and telecommuting hours, an amalgam of face-to-face exchanges, mediated communications (technologies *mediate* communication by imposing their own structure and environment), and stored-and-forwarded communications such as posted mail, voice mail, e-mail, or facsimile.

Here, the theoretical issues of organizational communications give way to practical considerations: What kinds of communication technologies are available and what are they good for? What types of face-to-face meetings are indispensable and which can be replaced by other forms of information sharing? What kinds of jobs are designed to handle day-to-day surprises (many managerial positions are) and would be compromised by telecommuting? How many in-office hours are necessary, how many can be replaced by telecommuting? Surely, answers to these concerns cannot be generated by sociological and communication theorems, but only by analysis of concrete organizational circumstance.

There is wide agreement that flexible work increases the need for formal communications; organizations that have trouble with formal information flow (and many do) will find themselves having to learn a new way of operating. Flexible work advocates make a good case that reliable, formal communication patterns are invaluable in any organization, flexible work arrangements notwithstanding. If flexible work is the excuse for putting them in place, they vouchsafe, so much the better. Indeed, some organizations use telecommuting strategies to improve coordination between managers and staff, and to implement new, efficient ways to communicate en masse to outside sales forces.[58]

Will an organization be willing to change its communication style to support flexible work? For managers accustomed to impromptu communication, flexible work arrangements get in the way. The telecommuters, however, may be fleeing constant interruptions and shifts in priorities that characterize impromptu discourse. If tensions arise between flexible workers and managers with spontaneous communication habits, they must be resolved for flexible work to endure.

There are basic communication tools and techniques that facilitate remote work. Well-orchestrated, regularly scheduled staff meetings are essential. Telecommuters must always be reachable and interruptible by telephone either through multiple lines, call waiting or a pager; we don't live in an environment where many secretaries place calls for their boss, and managers don't like to wait out a busy signal. Managers and co-workers need to be able to figuratively knock on the telecommuter's door when something comes up.

If an organization uses voice mail or e-mail, the telecommuter must periodically check for messages when working at home. Phone lists must be complete with home telephone numbers so telecommuters can be reached by one another as well as by their organizations. Monday morning memos and consolidated calendars should set forth weekly priorities, schedules, and work locations. In short, communication pathways between the remote worker and co-workers should be well defined and readily available.

Management by Objective

The change of moment when adopting flexible work is in management style. One executive bluntly explains the change: "We've decided to treat our employees as adults; supervision by observation has given way to supervision by results."[59]

The philosophy of managing employee results—management by objective (MBO)—rather than monitoring employee activity is not new: It was first popularized more than thirty years ago after adoption by the Pentagon. MBO has become accepted in most large corporations and in the U.S. military.

Just as uncompensated overtime at home was an unintended model of the telecommuting experience, managers of sales forces, dispersed field-service departments, messengers and other remote workers have shown over many years that since their activity cannot be monitored, their results must be managed.[60] The exercise of authority over the details of the work process gives way to authority over accomplishment. The time, place, pace, and rhythm of work are no longer commanded and controlled to assert managerial status. They are instead adjusted to meet work goals in the most productive manner.

In other terms, MBO supervises output (results) rather than input (ways of working, time, work space, etc.).[61] Instead of running a company as if it were a high school study hall, where observations of behavior take on more significance than learning, it is run like a college course; product, not process, is the final examination. Managers supervise employees the way they themselves are usually managed. The telecommuting transcriptionist picks up tapes of correspondence on Thursday afternoon; Friday afternoon she modems her documents back to the office for printing and signature. Her work is fully accounted, and she is fully accountable.

What is new in MBO is its application to flexible work. MBO is the management method that makes flexible work practical. In organizations that already manage objectives rather than activity, the adoption of flexible work is easier than in organizations that don't. Management has to go through fewer changes. Similarly, organizations that have a dictatorial and autocratic culture resist flexible work far more than those whose business culture is facilitative and cooperative.[62]

Narrowly construed, MBO can take the form of literal commands issued to staff about what they are supposed to accomplish by when. Organizations oriented towards flexible work look at MBO differently. They see it as a way of distributing responsibility. MBO is, for them, a process of setting goals, scheduling their dates of completion, and measuring worker contributions according to their quality and timeliness. Effective MBO is supportive, collegial, and consultative; the relationship between superior and subordinate provides for greater autonomy and results in improved quality of work.[63]

MBO is intended, especially in large organizations, as a method by which managers work with subordinate managers rather than a way of supervising line staff. In theory, supervisors could emphasize control or they, too, could seek to build commitment among their staff to organizational objectives. In the context of a flexible work program, however, MBO empowers telecommuters and flextime workers as well as traditionally scheduled employees throughout the organizational chart with personal responsibility and reasonable discretion for their work processes.[64] It presumes the extension of an MBO style to the whole organization.

A Pacific Bell vice-president, John Seymour, recommends the MBO challenge which any manager or supervisor would be wise to try:

> . . . When you go back to work, pick one of your subordinates with whom you think you are very clear in terms of what is expected. Take a blank piece of paper, hand it to the employee and ask him over the

next ten minutes to write down what he believes you expect. You do the same. You will find out how clear you are, or you aren't, very, very quickly when you take both of those pieces of paper and compare them. In . . . telecommuting, a substantial management challenge is to get very, very clear . . . expectations.[65]

In a study of an organization's telecommuting program, one manager explained the change he experienced:

"Telecommuting has helped me rethink my attitude toward supervision and how work should be done. You should just communicate your expectations, and if they are met, it doesn't matter how. I'm taking the performance agreement concept very seriously."[66]

Depending on the complexity of jobs, product turnaround, and employee positions, objectives can be defined with varying specificity. However, sometimes the difference between managing professional projects and clerical products is exaggerated. If a professional is expected to write a major report, her manager should break the project down into meaningful milestones so weeks don't pass before the professional's progress and difficulties come to light. By the same token, a clerical worker paid an hourly rate need not have hourly goals; perhaps productivity is best gauged as a aggregate of five or ten days of effort.

Some flexible work arrangements are compromised when anxious managers reassert management by control even while using the rhetoric of management by objective. One group of telecommuters had to write a memo explaining what they would do on their next telecommute day and then another memo the day after stating what they did. No such requirement was imposed on non-telecommuters. These very upset flexible workers needed to meet privately with an outside facilitator before the stressful and unnecessary memos were abandoned.

On the other hand, managers need to be aware of problems that prevent an employee who is telecommuting from completing an assignment. These are problems that have nothing to do with remote work, but snags that might afflict anyone in the office. An on-site worker who runs into obstacles is more likely to get the attention of a supervisor or co-worker. Managers need to schedule a time and place to assist remote workers with difficulties they are having.

Telecommuting and flextime do not eliminate the inefficiencies, interdependencies, and interruptions of one assignment by another that affect performance in any organization. Furthermore, in the first stages of telecommuting when management is apt to be least secure about the program, some loss of productivity is likely as employees adjust to their new roles. The prospects for collision rather than collusion should be recognized and given some time to work themselves out. An open, collegial, and communicative approach by management is the antidote.

Remote Management is Competent Management

Fundamentally, managing flexible workers need not be different from managing conventional workers. Good communications, careful definitions by management of its expectations of what will be completed when, and relationships with employees based on mutual respect are hallmarks of good management in any environment. They are also the attributes of successful flexible work management. Certain practicalities, such as effective electronic communication, bear on managing employees working at a distance, but only as an extension of a management style used on-site.

Conclusion

The selection and management of flexible workers is flexible work. It is more the employer in action than the employee. The employer has added new dimensions to his or her resources in choosing to manage employee time and space in a more thoughtful, productive manner. By understanding employee position and productivity, an employee is selected for the most appropriate form of flexible work. By undertaking this task on a meaningful scale, the employer maximizes returns. Uncertainty about telecommuting reveals itself as an untoward focus on employee personality, performance, or status. Some positions require more on-the-job experience than others to function well remotely; a few positions may be amenable to full-time telecommuting, although the vast majority will not. The most objective criteria for selection is the nature of the job, its telecommutability. This criteria ignores the status differences between clerical and professional workers.

Telecommuting programs fail to launch because of narrow selection processes; they fail to fly because of inappropriate management. While individual telecommuters sometimes need to be recalled, a program will generally succeed if it is well managed. Managers need to manage by objective if they are to give up managing purely by line of sight. They need to support telecommuting arrangements with appropriate technology and an insistence on cooperation among those who work together. Effective communication between telecommuters, managers, and nontelecommuters is the essence of cooperation. Perhaps the most remarkable aspect of managing telecommuters, employees at remote work centers, and those on flextime schedules is that it is really little different than managing well.

7

The Technologies of
Flexible Work

Remote work arrangements and sometimes even flextime are so
identified in the popular press with information technology
and telecommunications that it is often hard to tell where the technology ends and the work begins. The blurring is understandable.
Though entirely distinct resources, technology and flexible work
attract one another like mutually orbiting stars. As the John Hancock Insurance Company management found out, sometimes technology even pulls a staff into a flexible work orbit. Helping to set a
trend, the company wrote a computer program to distribute information to its clients electronically, to benefit managers of the
groups insured. The project catalyzed telecommuting.

John Hancock needed beta sites, that is, users to test the new system. They realized that the best prototype of Starview was the installation of access terminals in homes of experienced employees.
These were users whose in-home environments simulated the remote desktops of the outside benefit managers for whom Starview
was crafted. As employees, they could note bugs and other problems in the system before it became public. The constant after-
hours "play" with Starview by John Hancock professionals put
Starview through its paces, but it also taught employees about
telecommuting. They pointed out that the system not only distributed information; it had to accept information as well in order to
function. Underwriters could work remotely as well as their clients.
A flexible work program resulted. The technology functioned, as it

were, as a midwife to flexibility.[1] Later, the program collapsed when home-based computing failed to get support.

Remote work is fundamentally tied to information technology. Information must flow from a person in one location to a person or group in another location. Too often, however, such concepts simplify the underlying relationship between technology and remote work into a plug and play fantasy, a kind of "Have computer, will telecommute" Western. In this oversimplified view, everything technological is cheaper, easier, better—and ready to bring the work to the worker. It's the "can-do stuff" of the 1990s. For example, Link Resources, a flexible work research firm, proposed that:

> . . . Communications and computer technologies are now widespread and affordable enough so that managers can add many . . . categories of jobs that . . . function effectively and productively 'on the outside.' Telework has become a work-world reality.[2]

Work schedule will become entirely personalized. "It's a movable feast" exclaims Thomas Cross, a usually measured computer writer, declaring that "companies, spurred by the array of sophisticated new communications and computerized equipment, extend . . . automated offices' communications networks to include the telecommuter."[3] Routinely, an formidable list of technologies and services are anointed as necessities. What, you say you don't have a fax modem in your home office? Better get one quick!

Their reply to those who observe the relative scarcity of telecommuters? "You'll see!" As information technologies become more affordable, less user-surly, and more widely adopted, and as data and documents become more retrievable by computer, work at home is predicted to become commonplace. Computer technology will push telecommuting the way the roads defined the American commuter.

What undermines these expectations of technologically transformed work is the truism that technical feasibility does not assure that an organization will adopt technology, change the way workers work, or change work processes. Organizational and job changes that can magnify technology's return on investment regularly get overlooked, if not altogether neglected. Technology's usefulness depends upon the organization that acquires it.[4]

Organizations, even in the midst of a rapidly evolving technology marketplace, will not automatically support remote work arrangements, no matter how functional or low-cost technologies have become. Sure, the number of ad hoc arrangements spiral as so-called guerrilla telecommuters wheel and deal with their employers for technological backing. A flexible work program, however, is organized to promote systemic changes, to move beyond the limited incidence of solo adopters and dabblers.

Some flexible work proponents, perhaps in reaction to gadgetry, counter that high technology is not the issue, that technology is secondary to the adoption of remote work. Stressing the usefulness of widely available and very familiar technology, they emphasize POTS (Plain Old Telephone Service) over PANS (Pretty Advanced New Stuff).[5]

Pacific Bell's vice-president John Seymour, whose company is a telecommuting pioneer, explains:

> [Telecommuting] is something that can be done now. There is no new technology that needs to be invented. There are now new engineers that we need to bring out of school. Everything is here today in order to be able to do it. From a business perspective, one of the very nicest parts about it is that [telecommuting] is inexpensive, it is easy to implement.[6]

Many successful telecommuters do, in fact, work remotely with nothing more sophisticated than a conventional telephone. Outside sales forces having been working remotely this way for fifty years. We all know top executives, physicians, lawyers, government leaders whose *personal* technology is not much more sophisticated, even if they do have a desktop computer plainly visible and the staff to handle technicalities. The role of POTS, however, erodes as other, more functional technologies become familiar; the talented telephone system has evolved well beyond basic voice service. New technologies are making remote work easier to set up and more manageable.

The Economics of Flexible Work Technology

Many managers and organizations shy away from extensive telecommuting programs because of the costs of computers and telecommunication services such as telephone line charges and long distance tolls. Yet, flexible work arrangements can leverage *existing* investments in information technologies by extending their scope and usefulness. There may be no more cost-efficient way to squeeze additional value from in-house telecommunication and computers systems than by using extensions to support remote work arrangements. Flexible work arrangements marginally increase technology budgets, especially when compared to their payback in productivity. Because technological extensions efficiently build on investments, they are almost always inexpensive relative to the cost of the technological infrastructure being extended.

For example, the underlying economy of the immensely popular 800-toll-free line takes advantage of already established business telephone systems, order-entry systems, or other reception or service facilities that would still be in place without 800-lines, but would serve a smaller customer base. Similarly, the cost of opening access to an office's local area network (LAN) to remote workers is a fraction of original installation costs. Since some 60 percent of all business computers are now connected to LANs, the ease, cost, and efficiency of remote computing has increased significantly.

The costs of extending technologies to remote work sites can be managed economically. For example, a day's worth of data-entry activity can be compressed into a file and transmitted at a high data rate from a home or center in a single, efficient burst. Electronic mail can dramatically mitigate the cost of long distance communications between a telecommuter and her headquarters. Or, a telecommuter can take advantage of time zones and off-peak telephone pricing by starting work earlier than the standard eight to five shift (in the West for calls to the East) or working later than five (in the East for calls to the West).

In home-based telecommuter programs, many costs can be prorated between the employee and the employing organization. Even bigger-ticket items such as computers can be employee purchases. In technologies as well as organizational overhead, flexible work arrangements are potentially bargains for the employer.

Telecommunications leverages computer expenditures because the marginal cost of distributing information is a small fraction of the cost of creating it. To the extent an organization has already paid the bill for computer data, increases in data value as it is more widely used more than recoup the cost of distribution. Information basically costs nothing to duplicate, and costs very little to disseminate.

Move information to those who can use it most productively. It's not free, of course, but nothing of value is. As a consequence, even modest stretching of a company's technology to support flexible work increases the value of an organization's information; that increase is reflected in productivity.

How Telecommunications Leverages Computing

Among all technological resources, telecommunications defines the usefulness of the information technology (IT) infrastructure. Information requires movement in order to be useful, as Massachusetts Institute of Technology electrical engineer Claud Shannon proved in 1948. Without movement, information gathers dust like an unused library book. Computing is the shaker, but telecommunications is the mover. The technologies of flexible work move information to locations such as the home, once considered out of bounds.

Despite the rapid decline in the price of computer hardware, the total cost of institutional computing—software, housing, maintenance, programming, insurance, security, disposables such as paper and laser printer cartridges, electricity, depreciation, and obsolescence (especially!)—is almost invariably many times more costly than its telecommunications. The quantity of data that networks can move per second is rising geometrically while the cost per second remains relatively stable or increases only gradually. Even telephone-intensive industries, such as telemarketing firms, must press expensive computing systems into service.

The ratio between these two costs is not well understood because both computing and communications expenditures tend to be booked in all kinds of accounts, putting them and their comparison out of view. For example, in an interview with 80 executives from 46 leading service companies, 89 percent reported capitalizing computer hardware while 83 percent expensed infrastructural costs such as telecommunications.[7] Telecommunication costs rarely exceed 3 percent of total operating budget while computing costs run from 18 to 60 percent of operating costs.

As a consequence, extending computing resources to remote worksites uses the comparatively low-cost resource, telecommunications, to amplify a comparatively high-cost resource, computing.

Electronic mail over the Internet is a case in point. The cost of moving electronic mail is minor compared to the computing infrastructure that creates, stores, and receives messages. This information superhighway, even when tolls are established, costs an employer very little.

Certain kinds of computing organizations—enterprise-wide database management systems—are efficiently centralized, but become most effective when access to them is distributed. Useful data flows readily into the database, especially from point-of-sale systems, customer service centers, or other data-creating encounters, and flows back from the database to these locations, to analysts, accounting departments, and other users with distinct data interests. It is just such an approach that structures JC Penney's successful remote work program. For years, full-time, home-based telecommuters have provided customer services and order-taking for the retailer. Incoming 800-calls are routed to telecommuters using terminals connected to the company's mainframes. No customer is the wiser, but turnover among telecommuters is virtually nil.

Distributed information systems are possible because, for all of the diversity of technologies in use, information systems communicate with one another reasonably well. Even IBM, once famed for its proprietary communication protocols, touts the capacity of different machines to exchange data. International boundaries are crossed with electronic alacrity in banking, law enforcement, diplomacy, computer-automated design (CAD), financial markets, transportation and shipping, publishing, engineering, and other sectorial-based information exchanges.

The sender's information increasingly can be converted automatically to be intelligible to the information tools of the receiver; technological disparities between sender and receiver are mitigated. For example, an individual can write electronic mail and send it to a fax machine. Conversely, a computer equipped with a fax modem and optical character recognition can receive a fax and import the document into a word processor for editing, and fax it back. On the road, an electronic mail user can hear e-mail on the telephone, the text translated by a computer into speech. A report written on a computer running Windows software can be sent by modem to a Macintosh, where it will appear reasonably well formatted as a Macintosh file—and sent back again to the originating computer to continue preparation. The smooth flow of information between remote and office technologies becomes less costly as lower-end products on the remote side are good enough to work with higher-end products on the office side.

In large part, the momentum of the Information Revolution reflects the evolution of the telephone system. The usefulness of the ordinary telephone connection keeps improving as new techniques push larger volumes of data per second through the line. Indeed, a wonderful diversity of data can be transmitted: spreadsheets, faxes, voice messages, text messages, pictures, database entries, animation, or schematics. The simple hookups of a telephone line to a modem and a modem to a computer, and easily mastered communications software creates many new dimensions of information transmittal. (When the Chinese shut down satellite access to foreign journalists during the Tiananman Square uprising, clever technicians transmitted photographs via telephone to U.S. news outlets.)

Until recently, one roadblock to technologically advanced telecommuting has been the speed at which computer data could be transmitted to homes and remote work centers without expensive, custom installations. But now in major urban and suburban areas the most advanced telephone network for residential, small business, and remote work center use, the Integrated Services Digital Network (ISDN), is becoming available. This service provides a high data rate, 64,000 bits per second or better, on tariffs for installation, basic monthly fee, and use. Regional telephone companies have ISDN construction projects in their pipelines and more are coming.

Any organization that needs high data rates to the home can afford ISDN. ISDN service can meet nearly all communication requirements of any telecommuter or remote work center prevalent today where large amounts of data—CAD/CAM is the familiar example—must be moved. Alternative systems—from cable to satellite—offer interesting competition and the winners are far from selected. What seems certain is network capacity, at least in urban and suburban areas.

With higher data rates accessible, off-premise, home-based and center-based telecommuters can duplicate the kinds of computer communications they are accustomed to using on company premises. Large documents, graphic documents, and huge programs can be moved between home and office the way they are routinely moved within an office or between corporate facilities.

Productivity

Just as flexible work technologies leverage computing investments, they leverage personnel investments by increasing worker productivity. Consider a manager who, thanks to the computer, can digest much more information before making a decision than she did when information was harder to get. The decision may be more astute, but it may take considerably longer to reach than when she had less information to analyze. If managerial productivity is measured by decisions per hour, it is now lower for this individual situation.[8] Can, though, this manager delegate decision-making to others because information is distributed? Then decisions per hour (as a whole) might increase to boost managerial productivity, *even though individual productivity at some levels have lowered*. Organizations that rely on flexible work arrangements benefit from productivity gains of more decentralized decision-making.

There are few worker-proof information systems. Information technologies do not automatically generate bottom-line productivity gains if they are not consistent with the way people work, the tasks before them, or the organization in which they function. A top-line expenditure, investment in technological is necessary but not sufficient to increase productivity. Additional further investments are required.

For instance, jobs must be redesigned to harvest productivity increases from technological innovations. In many offices, the personal computer sitting clumsily on a desk designed for the typewriter tells a story. The technology is in the room, but it is probably not yet well-structured into the job.

More fundamental than furniture is how jobs should change as a result of new information technology. Often, personnel responsible for designing an information system barely talk to people using it; job applications are overlooked. Sometimes, technologies are almost thrown at work with disappointing results. Across the United States, for example, secretaries struggle with ersatz databases fashioned inside word processing or spreadsheet software. Their roles as list managers and their need to use genuine database applications have been neglected. They are textually harassed. A larger-scale example is found in the proliferation of different software packages providing the same function in different departments; this predicament is endemic in the public sector where agency upon agency invents its own unique solution to a common computer problem. A pointless inconsistency, it dramatically inflates the cost of training, data sharing, and technological upgrades. If technological planning were job-centered, the questions would be asked, "how can this job be optimized using IT? How can this department be optimized?" In that framework, the extension of technology to support flexible work arrangements becomes just the way to optimize performance.

How does technology fit into flexible work programs? Consider the VeriFone Corporation, a small company by industrial standards, but in profile, growth, and market share a very big company indeed.[9] VeriFone provides credit card authorizations via card reading terminals that one sees in stores everywhere. It regularly beats major players such as AT&T and IBM in bid contests around the world.

VeriFone has designed a very unusual organizational chart. The Chief Information Officer, Will Pape, is also in charge of human resources. This is an extraordinary positioning of a CIO. In most organizations, information systems are dominated by finance departments, report to a comptroller, or are organized as in-house enterprises that sell IT and telecommunication services to other departments. In government and education, especially, information systems are typically controlled by the finance department. These structures reflect the original use of IT for so-called bean counting functions such as accounting; bean-counting continues to be an important application of IT, but today is it only one among many.

In positioning its Chief Information Officer to integrate employees and technology, VeriFone put to rest the lingering industrial notion that technology should harness people by turning this anachronism on its head. People should harness IT. IT priorities should be set by human resource priorities. For example, VeriFone monitors the utilization of computer reports. If a report doesn't get requested often, it is dropped. In how many companies are there reports consuming tons of paper that no one reads? By the way, CIO Pape does his job from home, a thousand miles from corporate headquarters and about 500 miles from the nearest VeriFone office. And no, he doesn't own an airplane, just a computer.

VeriFone integrates various work arrangements—telecommuting, field-based sales staff, and traditional office organization—by using a computer-based communications web that ties them altogether. It bans paper memos for internal communication, and "forwardly deploys" staff people (one-third travel more than half the year) to puncture new markets. Off-the-shelf hardware and software provides VeriFone with electronic mail to manage work and organize collaborative efforts among a dispersed workforce. A typical manager receives sixty messages a day—wherever in the world she is at the moment.

The results are impressive. For example, the company assembles business proposals in a few days (while competitors take weeks) by using the "relay race paradigm." Work is handed off electronically among teams in different time zones across continents; the effect is a twenty-four-hour/day production cycle without overtime or loss of sleep. CIO Will Pape says the company is not structured around remote work because it happens to sell technological systems. "A toothpaste company could operate the same way."

Technological Parity

Headquarters is a communications channel, and more. It is where workers meet their work, tools, and materials. Tools and materials make working possible. Perhaps they use a terminal and an online database or have an adding machine and a pile of invoices to process. The practical technology of remote work duplicates or accesses work, tools, and materials. A telecommuter often needs a home computer because he uses a computer at work. Often, a telephone is not enough for more than occasional telecommuting for this reason.

There is no right technology for telecommuting; a wide diversity of technologies support flexible work arrangements. As technologies take hold in offices, they become more important to remote workers. For example, departmental purchases of facsimile machines have skyrocketed; most information workers use them at their jobs so it is helpful to be able to send a fax when telecommuting.

Skeptics observe that it took twenty years for the chip-based facsimile machine to catch on widely. Alas, facsimile transmission of photographs (then called wire photos) were common in newspaper offices by the early 1930s. Why did take it so long to for facsimile to spread? High cost? The dreadful ammonia smell produced by nondigital machines? Their bulk? Even today, administrative workers wildly overestimate the cost of sending a facsimile; they consider it equivalent to the cost of a telegram (a dollar or more), rather than a cost comparable to that of a photocopy. The machine's potential is still not well understood![10,11]

More generally, *parity* defines the relation between remote technology and office technology. The controlling factor in remote work is not, as is so often presumed, what gadgets the would-be telecommuter has at home or the elegance of the remote work center's technological resources, but what systems are used in the office. A fitfully automated organization cannot support remote work which is highly computerized. An organization which depends on sophisticated telecommunication and data processing systems will disadvantage the telecommuter who is unable to log onto these systems remotely. In short, if there is an actively used facsimile at the office, it does makes a difference if there is one at home or nearby.

An old saw in high school physics declares that water seeks it own level. Perhaps you recall the oddly shaped glassware used to demonstrate this principle. Similarly, technology seeks its own level not only in remote applications, but throughout an organization. As technological innovations are added, they tend to diffuse over time much as ink diffuses when added to a container of water. Remote work opens a new channel of diffusion.

In the dynamic view of remote work, technology is approached positively, but not prescriptively; there is no "should" or "must."[12] Rather, the following principles govern the balance between technology and flexible work organization:

- Regardless of its technological level, any organization can implement effective flextime and flexiplace arrangements.
- As the technological level evolves, the potential scope and scale of remote work evolves in parallel.
- Remote work becomes more productive to the degree that remote technologies replicate the office environment, substitute for it, and communicate from a distance with it.

Different technological levels among organizations rarely foreclose remote work. A flexible work program needs to assess the tools and materials requirements of activities proposed for telecommuters. That almost by itself guides the telecommuter to appropriate technologies. The industrial component of remote work is important when repetitive production characterizes a job (as, for example, is true of data entry positions). However, unlike machines of gears and ratchets, contemporary digital communications and computing systems have the flexibility, size, and pricing to accommodate remote work arrangements. Furthermore, all of these technologies travel well; their portable variations can be used in cars, some airplanes, most hotel rooms, and nearly any company office; they allow a class of remote workers to move between home-based, office-based, remote office-based, and in-between, travel-based telecommuting.

The parity principles are good news to the manager contemplating flexible work, but put off by the possibility of an expensive, blind date with IT. The arrangement is unlikely to be costly. Similarly, there should be few surprises in the suite of required technologies. There will be new computing and telecommunication subsystems that need to be installed and managed to facilitate remote work, but like offspring they will share the character, functionalities, and approximate complexity (or less) of the in-house systems to which they tie.

In the simplest of situations, the remote technology might be a telephone credit card, a simple device that borrows the billing capability of a commercial telephone company. Slightly more involved extensions, such as remote access to computing systems through a LAN or dial-up connections to a mainframe database, will still retain a relative simplicity compared to the systems being extended. This equation is not the least bit mysterious. One can generally find a prototype of remote access within an in-house system. For example, a company that is distributing mainframe data to different offices within a facility is already supporting work remote from the computer. The technical challenges of moving this data off-premise are not significant in comparison. It is likely that an organization is already using systems with built-in remote access capabilities that can be activated; nearly all LAN software, for example, can be readily upgraded for this purpose.

Technical Challenges

Where technology is a problem in a remote work program is not in the setup but in support. Imagine a telecommuter working with a computer that suddenly goes dark. Was the power cord accidentally pulled, or did the monitor fail, or did software crash as it sometimes does for inexplicable reasons? On-site there is usually someone around who can be called in. At a distance, diagnosing even a simple problem can be hard, especially if the telecommuter is unskilled technically and doesn't know trouble-shooting. One company always has a telecommuter use a terminal and a modem in-house before setting up at home so a technician can provide direction and suggest responses to typical failure points.

Telecommuting arrangements usually define a maximum number of hours in which technical problems must be resolved—or the telecommuter must return to the office, perform other work, or debit vacation leave. Nonetheless, gaps in support for computers and telecommunications faced by telecommuters (and sometimes by flextimer workers if they work at off-shift hours when support is unavailable) can impair a program. Technical support requirements must be evaluated when organizing a telecommuting program. The level of financial and technical support available must be adequate to keep remote technology up and running.

Training challenges may arise. In a very small organization the use of a modem, say, for remote access to a stand-alone computer may represent a brand new application. Where workers are self-taught, there may not any prior experience with computer communications. Perhaps there is a need to connect one kind of home computer to another kind of office computer. One might need a consultant's help; still, the problems to solve are quite modest in this setting.

Larger organizations sometimes have a harder time than smaller organizations supporting remote IT not because of greater complexity to their infrastructures, but because their technology organization may have management problems that makes doing anything new difficult. The failure of the Hartford Insurance Company telecommuting program mentioned at the beginning of this chapter illustrates how the lack of technical support can even cripple a telecommuting program.[13]

In that company, unsuitable telecommunication linkages were

patched together for a telecommuting program. When they failed to perform adequately, remedies were frustrated because accountability for network operations was scattered among five different company groups; no one group accepted responsibility for making remote access for telecommuting dependable. Although a lack of top management support ultimately doomed Hartford's program, technical problems were the beginning of its end.

In another example, a small, nonprofit organization's few loanable computers and modems severely limited professional participation in a telecommuting pilot. There, hardware limitations were compounded by a constrained telecommunications budget and a reimbursement procedure (60 percent of the telecommuter's telephone bill) which discouraged outbound communication from the home.[14] While the pilot was a success from a commute-reduction perspective, telecommuting died out for want of IT funding.

For professionals, the biggest problems with telecommuting arise because of missing tools and materials (typically computer workstations or information resources) rather than communications. Communications can be deferred or handled by telephone; without hardware and information, however, professionals may twiddle their thumbs as any other workers would without materials to process or tools to process them. For clerical workers, the remote site must have the equivalent of office tools and materials or telecommuting is impossible. Professionals usually have the advantage of more varied forms of work than clerical workers; for them even simple tools and materials—reports to read and edit—can support occasional telecommuting.

Networks can transmit information resources, but many telecommuters tuck a few diskettes in a briefcase and sling loaner laptop computers over their shoulders. However, the more advanced an organization's IT, the more information can be accessed electronically. Most professional work generates unanticipated information needs. To transfer documents or look up data remotely on the fly, without prior planning or asking the office to retrieve and fax something, is valuable. Even highly advanced organizations, however, do not place all information online; professionals have to plan carefully what they must have at home on telecommute days—and, if possible, have some help available by telephone to retrieve hardcopies.

Information Security

If the telecommuter worries about technological reliability, the organization often worries about technological security. Some companies have discouraged telecommuting because of their security concerns.[15] Private computer systems, no matter how sensitive their applications, have time and time again shown themselves susceptible to hacking, perusal of confidential information, embarrassing or detrimental breaches of private records, and even high tech vandalism. Even public telephone systems and defense systems are not invulnerable. For this reason, office systems are sometimes kept closed; they cannot be accessed except by terminals from within the office.

However systems become much more vulnerable because they are open, hackers, notwithstanding all of the publicity they generate, are not the big problem. In a GAO study of thirty-five abuses of federal information systems, *all* were traced to disgruntled current or former employees who had ready access to the systems they violated.[16] Most security threats derive from inattention to security issues or from employee breaches rather than from trespass by outsiders.

A telecommuting program may, for the first time, open a company system to off-site access. A variety of hardware and software approaches can be implemented to limit open systems to authorized users, and to limit authorized users to authorized uses. The price of a well-developed information technology network should incorporate the expertise and subsystems needed to secure it from attack or misuse. These include, for example, levels of password protection, data encryption, call-back routines that control the telephone lines allowed to connect to a system, dedicated lines that obviate dial-up access, and logging systems that track system users and what they do. Even banks are comfortable providing remote access by telecommuters; they use data encryption technologies to scramble telephone lines, sophisticated computerized password systems, and "adequate locks on home-office facilities."[17] Technological safeguards must be paralleled by emphatic, heavily promoted policies that spell out to users their responsibilities for information security. Rules must control, limit, or prohibit removal of sensitive hardcopy (such as a personnel folder) from company premises.

The most common and expensive form of hacking is not of databases, but of telephone systems. Direct Inward Dialing or DID is a feature option found in many large PBX installations (company telephone systems); DID allows a user to call into the PBX and, from there, make outbound calls at a better rate than can be obtained residentially. It is obviously useful to remote workers. Generally, the liability for unauthorized DID falls on the operator of the PBX. Companies have been hit hard by freeloaders; one even went out of business because of DID charges. Tracing DID thievery can be fruitless. PBX owners need to carefully compare the risks of DID to the toll savings it confers on legitimate calls.

Choosing Optimal Technologies for Remote Work

Sorting out the computing and telecommunication needs of a contemporary organization is as much an art as a science. In part, the panoply of technolgies for storing and transmitting information creates ambiguous trade-offs in cost, functionality, ease of use, and capacity between them. Selecting the optimal suite of information technologies is a difficult challenge. With many well-priced IT options available to small bsuinesses, small size no longer relieves an organization of the burden of carefully procuring and managing its technology resources.

The principles of technological parity and extension enumerated above provide a starting point when equipping remote workers with technology; they help to narrow the issues that an organization must consider, but they do not prescribe a unique technological solution to working remotely. Yet another factor must be scrutinized, namely, organizational *style*. Consider the experiences of GTE, the nation's largest local exchange carrier. Like all telephone companies, GTE avidly and inevitably pursues the telecommuting marketplace; some compensated work is done in 40 percent of the households it serves. It advertises telecommuting, consults on work-at-home technologies through toll-free advice lines, and has even developed a new kind of telephone for this market called TeleGo, a compact cobination of a cordless and a cellular phone that works at home and on the road

GTE found that telecommuters come to remote technlogy (and to GTE!) in their own way, at their own pace. Telecommuting promotions generate many customer inquiries but few sales. Now GTE focuses on responding to six basic communication issues raised by telecommuting: (1) ready telephone contact with key individuals; (2) maintenance of a professional image; (3) accessibility; (4) computer communications; (5) mobile communications; (6) teleconferencing.

These issues help sift through remote technologies. For example, if customers of yours will be calling a home-office, note that the sounds they hear add to their image of your business. Do your telecommuters need a professional sounding voice mail system, or will an answering machine suffice? Use these issues to formultate the communication environment needed by your telecommuters; you'll shop smarter if you do.

Conclusion

The information infrastructure created by the computer greatly enriches the contents of communications. Mighty storage capacity, blazing microprocessors, physical compactness, and overall reductions in price have transformed computing. Changes at the PC level are exponentially reflected in dramatic improvements in super workstations, minicomputers, and mainframe computers.[18] As a result, there is a catalyzing swell in the complexity of data that can be processed and stored at remote sites.

The principle of technological parity ensures that the technologies of remote work, in the context of the organization using them, will not swell budgets for equipment or communications excessively. The technical prowess required to establish technological links to the remote worker will remain relatively consistent with that already found in-house. Extensions of information and telecommunication systems to telecommuters are not likely to put the manager out on a limb.

Modern computers are versatile. With a few thousand dollars in a telecommunications budget, the remote computer offers alternatives to many face-to-face conversations as well as tools with which to write a report, calculate a spreadsheet, enter data to a database, design a computer chip or logo, and so forth. Computers crop up so often in telecommuting articles because they are boxes that nearly bring it all together.[19]

These combine, on the telecommunications side, with digital

networking, more favorable long distance telephone rates, robust networks, and better data throughput. Thus, capabilities of computers, linked by networks, create an entirely new information infrastructure in which data entry, processing, storage, and retrieval are more decentralized, independent activities.

More generally, evolving computer technology in tandem with evolving corporate and public telephone networks create a truly extraordinary capability to free work from spatial and temporal constraints. In this environment, workers no longer must necessarily commute to information to use it. It is quite possible for the lucky to work with few restraints on their location other than their employer. The factor of distance is tolerably well eliminated by telecommunications and low-cost personal computing.

Technology allows for accelerated spatial and temporal dispersion of work—to homes, to flexible hours, to remote work centers, and to travel and travel destinations. Work can be distributed geographically, and to people working at different times. More importantly, perhaps, tasks can be accomplished interdependently rather than dependently. Data entry can be organized at one remote work center, whereas financial analyses may be provided to data consumers in headquarters and homes all at once. Management conferences become low-cost audio conferences regardless of individual travel schedule or worksite.

In larger organizations, 80 percent of all telephone traffic is internal: The telephone is preferred even among people physically close to one another. Face-to-face communication has its rewards, especially in negotiations, but it also has limitations. For a great deal of work, especially the exchange of information, telecommunications is preferable. Calls, voice mail, and electronic mail are spontaneous (no advanced scheduling necessary), are pithy, can be declined, can be switched (call transfer) to another party or to voice mail, as a rule do not require knowledge of the other party's location, and allow parties simultaneous access to their computers, notes, and other resources they might not have in a conference room, but have at their offices and homes.

Remote work exploits these advantages. The more you look at the available, affordable technology of remote work, the less remote it seems.

II

Implementing Flexible Work

Step 1
Inaugurate a Broad Discussion of Flexibility Issues

Organizations considering flexible work learn much from a broad-based, internal dialog about work, family, success, and the values that give these issues shape. Often, the depth of productivity problems arising from traditional job structures are poorly recognized. Many organizations start planning flexible work by surveying work and care-giving conflicts, employee scheduling of leisure time, commuter hassles, and other problems that prompt interest in flexible work. A survey of employees and managers provides a good point of departure for change and allows common employee strains and worries to be assessed.

Organizations sometime hire outside facilitators to conduct focus groups of employees and managers, undertake surveys, or moderate a task force. Facilitators encourage candor in meetings and may break down stereotypical thinking ("only women need flexible hours" or "telecommuters can't be managed" or "personal lives should be left at the door"). Facilitators in closed-door meetings help engage the wary. Employees often fear they will prejudice their reputations by acknowledging work/family conflicts. The objective of the process is to uncover employee and management views, to identify issues that might sanction a flexible work program, and to open minds to the potential benefits of restructuring work hours and locations. Such discussions themselves bolster employee relations, but they also create expectations of change for which management should be prepared. The Du Pont corporation found this out when it surveyed 4,000 employees:

> "One word that cried out from the responses that we got back was flexibility—that one word in neon lights, popping off the pages of these surveys. They wanted flexibility in schedules, flexibility in where they could work, flexibility in benefits, flexibility of career planning. And that got everyone's attention. It was just an overwhelming response focused on a single issue."[1]

Step 2
Choose Flextime, Telecommuting, and/or Remote Work Centers

An organization begins to organize flexible work by developing guidelines for acceptable changes. Guidelines provide initial answers to basic questions. Can work hours, work locations, or both be restructured? What kinds of jobs may be suited to alternative work arrangements? What resources will flexibility require and where might they come from? In organizational terms, who will lead the program? Is the organization prepared to invest in new remote work facilities? Have a concept put together by people with imagination and a thorough grasp of the organization's culture, structure, activities, and capacity for change.

Flextime, the most widely adopted and well-understood form of flexible work, appeals for implementation. Only one employee in ten at Bell Atlantic is not working a flextime schedule.[2] Organizationally, flextime programs are straightforward to implement: They do not disturb most benefits of a common workplace and they resemble shift assignments. Even single shift organizations have people who come early or leave late; there is already something of a bandwidth for flextime. And because flextime shares some of the challenges and benefits of telecommuting, it helps to prepare an organization for more complex flexible work arrangements. An organization that did not include flextime in its program would be unusual among those serious about flexible work.

Telecommuting arrangements, apart from a limited number of deals with individuals, require more effort to launch, and offer more dramatic benefits. A commitment to telecommuting can be more problematic for management. Telecommuting, however, can be implemented slowly; individual arrangements may be six months in the making after a program begins. An organization can agree to a wide examination of telecommuting potential by soliciting applications and granting case-by-case approvals. Implementation can crawl in an organization that likes to work that way. The best way to resolve telecommuting in an organization with many doubts is to learn how it works on a small scale. In that context, telecommuting is always viable.

Developing Remote Work Centers

Remote work centers are time-consuming to organize and, compared to flextime and home-based telecommuting, the most expensive. Furthermore, remote work centers are successful where their charters closely fit the geography, budget, and activities of participating organizations. Their development is hard to describe in general terms. Facility costs drive remote work center development.

The first steps in organizing a remote work center are analytical. Determine:

- costs of remote work facilities compared to headquarters space
- potential gains in productivity
- potential increases in retention of workers
- potential access to new labor markets
- commute impact

These results may be surprisingly favorable.

At present, the dedicated remote work center or satellite work center, used exclusively by a single organization, seems most promising. Different organizations have a hard time using space cooperatively. However, this conclusion is still in trial in a number of government-sponsored, multiorganizational research projects and a consensus is not in place.

Unlike the branch offices they resemble, dedicated centers house more diverse activities and positions, have commute-related criteria for siting, and usually have different communication requirements because of their diversity. The first region in the United States, not surprisingly, to define the commute-reduction benefits of remote work centers was the Los Angeles air basin. There, the Air Quality District ruled that branch offices do not contribute to commute reduction goals required of larger companies, but remote work centers do. As commute reduction districts across the United States are obliged to implement the regulations of the Federal Clean Air Act, remote work centers could become popular among many corporations.

As a form of flexible work arrangements, remote work centers contrast with home-based telecommuting in that employees can be supervised on-site and, of course, work is performed at a company facility. For organizations uncomfortable with managing work performed at home, satellite centers may be more palatable.

Home-based telecommuting and flextime programs offer experience relevant to satellite work. Moreover, their objectives are similar. The tasks of starting home-based telecommuting and flextime programs are much simpler; telecommuting teaches organizations how to manage remote work centers without the center's comparatively high costs.

Nearly all of the stages required for home-based telecommuting reappear in organizing remote work centers. Commute reduction criteria (say, residential zip code) will partly define the potential of a remote work center by employees sharing a geographic area. However, within that number (which could be large), job-related criteria is used to select remote workers just as it is used to select home-based telecommuters.

While on-site supervision is available in a remote work center, it can be quite impractical for a particular supervisor to join a supervisee at a remote location. Thus, on-site supervision becomes more general, provided by someone who may have no other link to the employee than the center itself. A greater degree of independence among center employees is inevitable. Again, many issues carry over from home-based telecommuting and flextime programs.

Organizations interested in remote work centers can benefit by introducing home-based telecommuting and flextime. An organization will hone its management of flexible work and help tailor work center plans more precisely to the organization's goals and needs of the workforce.

Step 3
Set Short- and Long-Term Goals
for Participation

At their onset in organizations, flexible work programs have one of two sentiments guiding their rhetoric. They can be tentative pilots without any particular guarantee of lasting more than a few years. Numerous companies have organized telecommuting pilots that came and went, never to be heard from again. Or they can begin prototypes that anticipate that flexibility will take hold throughout the organizations sponsoring them. Like a pilot, a prototype has a beginning point and an ending point; that period becomes the subject of the evaluation. However, prototypes focus on finding the best ways to manage flexible work arrangements in the setting of a long-term commitment to flexibility.

As though following an unwritten law, many institutions initiate flexible work pilots. They resolve that subsequent evaluations will decide whether or not to carry on with flexible arrangements. For those who wonder if their organization should also put flexibility on trial, consider the number of academically supervised pilots concluding that flexible work, especially telecommuting, effectively increases productivity, reduces commute miles, improves employee satisfaction, and so forth.[3,4] In experiences recounted in earlier chapters, flexible work arrangements have testified to—if not proven—their mettle in reducing work-related conflicts for large groups of employees and in leveraging technology. The unanimity of verdict in investigations of flexible work gives little incentive to reprise them.

A practical reason for initiating a prototype is cost. Candidly, prototypes are much cheaper than serious pilots. In an authoritative pilot, expensive professionals are required to structure the experiment, set up data traps, and collect and analyze data scientifically. Substantial company time must be factored for record-keeping, survey completion, and in-depth interviews that are the foundations of rigorous, empirical social study.

There are fundamental differences between prototyping flexible work in a small organization and a large organization. Large organizations enjoy additional organizational layers (work groups, departments, divisions, etc.), diversity of job types in different units, and decentralized decision-making that make top-down implementation of flexible work ill-advised. An organization of ten, fifty, or even a hundred employees can make a common commitment to flexible work innovations. Larger organizations usually authorize flexible work in general management policy, but leave many aspects of implementation to departments to control.

Scale of the Prototype

An unsuccessful beginning might rob a program of its potential by discouraging future participation. Thus, wisdom lies with starting a prototype on a small scale, and limiting the number of departments and/or participants. Starting small has the obvious virtue of concentrating program resources, facilitating oversight, and limiting real or perceived risks.

Some organizations, including the state of California, call for prototypes of sufficient compass to involve a cross-section of job classifications, be generalizable to the department (or agency) as a whole, and assess "the satisfaction and productivity of staff who do not telecommute, as successful telecommuting is a team effort."[5] In this view, the purpose is not to see whether or not telecommuting (or flextime) works in some general sense, but to determine its viability for each department.[6] These parameters can help define a useful scale of participation.

In large organizations, it is tempting to limit a prototype to one or two divisions such as the information systems group or the outside sales force. However, the goal of a prototype is to set the stage for broad participation. If possible, plant many seeds for a larger harvest. Each employee group has a lesson to teach.

While there is no formula for deciding the scale of participation in a prototype, a handful of telecommuters is probably worth little except to the individuals participating. Further, economies of scale in program costs that otherwise accrue (in such elements as training, telecommunications, and computing) will be sacrificed. The United States is filled with corporations with official flexible work programs in which a marginal number of employees actually participate. Symbolic programs generate good press but reap few organizational or societal benefits, and they are certainly not instructive.

Departments should make the effort to calculate the flexible work potential of their staffs. These become reference points against which to measure numbers of staff who volunteer for flexible work, the numbers selected, and the numbers of those who actually maintain alternative work arrangements. In very large departments, the calculation of flexible work potential requires an onerous review of job descriptions. Without goals, however, participation might flatten unnecessarily because there would be no criteria by which to judge what could happen, but has not.

Program plans then define participation goals as percentages of flexible work potential. The literature envisions as many as 15 percent of the workforce eventually flexing work hours or work site; professional organizations may reach the goal of 20 percent of staff telecommuting at least twice monthly.[7] Among administrative, clerical, professional staff, a goal of 25 percent of the staff working remotely some portion of the month, and 50 percent on flextime schedules may even be feasible. Percentages of flextime participation could go much higher; in many companies, virtually the entire work force is on flextime schedules, with a small number choosing to start at eight A.M. and quit at five P.M.

Phased Implementation

Once the program is announced and promoted, its resources defined, and its expectations of departmental cooperation explained, an unpredictable number of departments and employees will volunteer to participate. If the response threatens to overwhelm program resources (say, the number of training sessions needed is more than the program can provide at the time), departments will have to form a queue. As soon as possible, departments in the wings should be added. More experientially oriented organizations may use the queue to diversify participation; departments of different sizes, mixes of positions, and roles can be picked.

Program planners will need to work closely with departments to evaluate the appropriate pace of implementation. Departments with high potential for flexible work arrangements and a large staff may need to phase participation in gradually to avoid being overwhelmed by changing work arrangements, technical issues, or the effort of learning how to manage by objective.

The Southern California Association of Governments (SCAG) pilot, subject to deeper and more capacious analysis than any other telecommuting pilot in America, has become something of a touchstone. SCAG recommends increasing participation over time—say, from 5 to 15 percent—so that the organization has "time to adequately adjust [to] the changes in work patterns and to obtain the necessary computers and software."[8]

Step 4
Assign an Individual or Group to Head the Program

A flexible work program must be organized by someone. In a small business with ten employees, the coordinator may be the owner. In an agency of 5,000 there may be a task force of twenty and a project staff of two or three. However large or small the organization and the number of flexible work participants, accountable staff must be assigned to the program; institutional leaders must meet to craft policy and set priorities. If the scope of the company's commitment is clear, day-to-day issues should be well within the scope of competent staff or consultants to address. A flexible work program cannot be organized by memoranda.

Because flexible work touches a number of issues—personnel, technology, facility management to name a few—flexible work programs are generally led by a committee or task force. It will include representative department-level managers and participants, as well as senior managers drawn from human resources, information systems, telecommunications, and public relations. As needed, counsel, space managers, accountants, and other specialists may be invited to the task force to address specific kinds of issues. If the task force becomes large, subcommittees and a small executive committee will expedite its work.

The task force needs staff who can carry out decisions and move about the organization to foster the program. It is impossible to calculate in advance the staff hours required to launch a flexibility program. To a degree, the pace of program implementation can be modulated to fit the staffing level the organization can afford; the danger is that once the program is heavily promoted, positive responses from departments will dissipate if the help they get from the organizing team is little and late. At a minimum, organizations of all sizes should designate at least a part-time coordinator. The key criteria for choosing a coordinator (besides availability) is access to and the confidence of top management.

The functions of the coordinator are straightforward:

- answer questions about the program
- provide technical and management support
- monitor progress
- assess benefits and costs
- conduct evaluations
- resolve problems[9]

As an alternative, independent consultants and management firms can be engaged to set up and run an entire flexible work program. For larger organizations, consultants are useful catalyst of change. They help define goals and keep the program moving. They also bring baggage. Anxious to put a successful program in place, some steer the selection of telecommuters or remote workers to the most trusted professionals, an approach that can severely limit participation. If management has a broader view of the scope and breadth of the start-up program—that it includes clerical workers, for example—it should direct its program consultants accordingly.

Organizations may balk at consultant fees and are often satisfied with a more informally structured, home-grown program. In the public sector, a number of large flexible work programs have hired consultants as fixed-term employees for twelve to twenty-four months. If the program is broad enough to keep a consultant-turned-employee busy, this approach is the most economical source of on-site, experienced support.

In a large, multilayered organization, program coordination will be seconded by departmental coordination assigned, typically, to administrative support personnel. They keep records of flexible work arrangements, assist in scheduling flextime and telecommute days, and work closely with the program coordinator to support their department's participants. In a highly diversified department with administrators, technical staff, and clerical staff, there may even be profit to assigning several coordinators. Each will assist a particular pool of employees.

Step 5
Define a Flexible Work Budget and Funding

A fter assessing employee needs, deciding on appropriate kinds of flexible work arrangements, establishing goals for participation, and appointing coordinators, the next step is to construct a budget for the program. The process identifies funding sources, defines and authorizes expenditures, and allocates costs between the organization and participating employees.

By and large, flexible work programs do not add significant new expenses or expose employers to increased risk. Of the expenses associated with flexible work, few are unique to flextime, telecommuting, or even satellite work centers. Except for technology, training, and possibly promotional expenses, direct costs are generally small. And these costs can be moderated to fit almost any budget. Some very large programs commit one or more full-time positions to coordination, but no more than they would to managing any large-scale change. Employers worry about increased risk as well. Fortunately, none of the standard employer risks—workers' compensation, in particular—increase solely as a consequence of flexible work arrangements.

In many instances, flexible work shifts costs, some up, some down. For example, an increase in telephone costs may be accompanied by a reduction in space costs. Accounting the financial gains and losses of flexible work can be elusive. Most organizations are content with a project budget and special analysis of estimated costs as part of a program's evaluation.

Given the difficulty of accounting the costs of flexible work, managements emphasize efficient consumption of variable resources such as telecommunications. Some costs are shared. Fixed costs, like promotion, evaluation, portable computers, or training are based on an organization's size, commitment to flexible work, technological level, and style. This chapter provides a wide-ranging template for planning a flexible work budget and anticipating costs that may be ongoing.

Identifying Funding Sources

Funds will generally be carried by the cost center that customarily pays for the type of expenditure at issue. If as a rule, for example, the personnel department pays for employee development then it should sponsor flexibility training. If a departmental budget generally covers technology, it can be expected either to pay for telecommuting technologies or apportion those costs to employees.

Exceptions, however, are sometimes made by companies who wish to prime the pump. Administrative or special project funds may be expended centrally for flexibility to encourage departmental participation. If flexibility is an innovation of top management, departments will expect augmentations to their budgets to cover costs they have not had to bear previously. Enterprise-wide services such as mainframe databases that need remote access by telecommuters would certainly be candidates for such support.

The human resource department or other administrative cost centers should bear certain flexibility costs because they need to be universally available and uniform in content. These costs include training, educational and promotional materials, model documents such as telecommuter agreements, one-time technology consultations, facilitators for focus groups and/or support groups, electronic bulletin board services, and program evaluation.

If these costs are pushed onto departments, there are several downsides. When departments make their own arrangements for training, for example, they may end up rehearsing employees for alternative work arrangements differently; the integrity of the program, however, depends on consistent content to training. Economies of scale of a single classroom would be sacrificed. Some departments would dispense with training altogether to save money.

Telecommuting would be encouraged by providing individuals or departments with equipment useful to remote work; however, the cost of providing a large amount of supportive technology, say, laptop computers, could skyrocket. Whether a company or agency curbing expenditures would significantly fund quantities of supplemental technologies is doubtful.

Budget Commitment

A budget for a flexible work program addresses eight kinds of costs: program management expenses, overhead expenses incurred by participating departments, security and utility costs generated by flextime schedules, general office expenses, data processing costs, telecommunications costs, document management expenses, and home office expenses. Only program, facility, and overhead expenses may incurred by flextime implementation, while telecommuting and flexiplace arrangements can incur costs in all categories.

Program management expenses are generated by the use of outside consultants, dedicated program coordinators, orientation and training sessions provided for participating departments, and program evaluation. Depending on how a program is organized and the number of employees participating in it, these expenditures can vary from a few hundred dollars to tens of thousands of dollars.

Departmental overhead encompasses the cost of managing telecommuters and flextime workers, monitoring costs incurred by telecommuters, the cost of processing reimbursements or disbursements associated with telecommuting activity, and training so highly specific to a department that it is not legitimately part of program management.

Security and utility costs arise from flextime because employees may be using buildings during periods of the day or night when few fellow employees are present, or when building air conditioning and heating systems are usually turned off to conserve energy. Flextime employees must also be safe as pedestrians.

Building security measures need not be itemized here; rather, the company should consider how off-shift workers may increase or change security requirements. Very large employers usually have evening escort services that can assist flextime workers working out-of-shift hours as they make their way to parking lots or mass transit. Smaller organizations may have to work hard to establish security. Perhaps flextime schedules can be coordinated so that groups of employees escort one another to their cars. Perhaps a security guard can assist individuals leaving work. If there are not be enough employees with comparable schedules, telecommuting instead of flextime or even a taxi driver who meets departing workers can be of assistance. In planning flexible work, consciousness of employee safety is important.

Similarly, planning needs to take into account heating, air conditioning, and lighting when work schedules change as a result of flextime. About 70 percent of flextime workers choose to start earlier than they would on a standard schedule, and about 30 percent choose to end their day later.[10] Since buildings are cold in the morning and hot in the evening, flextime can have definite implications for building utility costs. One flextime worker, working long into the evening when the air conditioning system was off, sweated onto computer disks damaging the delicate heads inside the computer! In a company with carefully managed, central heating and air, all building systems were set to start at 7 A.M. Flextime schedules beginning earlier required individual tuning of building systems. A flextime program will have to work with plant operations or the equivalent to find cost-effective environmental conditioning for off-shift uses. Workers may use individual heaters in the winter, but in hot climates there may be shift limits to avoid having to cool a whole building for a few hours for a few employees.

Building access, maintenance schedules of computers (when they become unavailable during data back-up, for example), off-peak air conditioning, and other mechanical rhythms of work may need to be reviewed and adjusted. In multitenant buildings with centralized heat and air, special arrangements with the building owner/manager may be needed. There are leases that restrict after-hour access that may need amendment. Program planners take the lead in discussing these issues with appropriate experts and advise the organization accordingly.

General office expenses should not differ from those incurred by nontelecommuting employees except where inventories are affected or where special stock is required for equipment peculiar to the telecommuting environment.

Data processing and telecommunications expenditures could, in theory, apply to a wide variety of hardware, services, and software. In practice, the items actually used by a telecommuter form a short list.

Telecommuting may engender document management expenses that the office does not. For example, a telecommuter may need use to an overnight courier service to send and receive materials to and from an office. Or, a fax machine may be necessary for the transmission of special forms, graphics, and so forth. This requirement could be met with home equipment, but usually a nearby facsimile service center is adequate. Similarly, document processing services (such as photocopying) may be acquired off-site from commercial firms.

Home office expenses are costs of the telecommuting environment additional to those described in the preceding categories. In this discussion, they include the allocation of residential space to office work, furniture such as chairs, desk, or computer stand, utilities needed by the telecommuter, and filing cabinets or other storage equipment.

The following suggests the range of possible budget categories:

Telecommuting Budget Categories and Potential Expense Areas

PROGRAM OVERHEAD

Consultants
Educational materials
Evaluation
Focus and support groups
Orientation sessions
Promotion
Program management: Coordinator(s); Task Force
Training sessions (all)
Work group meetings

SECURITY AND UTILITIES OF THE PREMISES

Air conditioning
Heating
Inside and outside lighting
Security personnel and equipment
Security procedures

DEPARTMENTAL OVERHEAD

Coordinator
Monitoring, Cost, Task, Benefits
Reimbursement processing
Scheduling and coordination
Software instruction
Technology support

GENERAL OFFICE

Forms
Supplies

DATA PROCESSING

Bulletin board service
Dial-up access
Desktop publishing systems
E-mail
Microcomputers and peripherals
Security systems: Encryption, Access protection
Software: Additional licenses, Manuals
Typewriter
User support (hot line)

TELECOMMUNICATIONS

Answering machine
Custom calling features
Facsimile/fax board
Fax/modem switch
Modem: standard, high-speed, answer-back
Paging
Surge protection
Telephone set

Telephone line: calling features, long distance service, type of
   local service, Centrex, leased, measured business, off-premise
   (OPX), residential, line conditioning
Tolls: credit card, reimbursed
Voice mail service

HARDCOPY DOCUMENT MANAGEMENT

Courier service
Facsimile service
Photocopying
Postage

HOME OFFICE

Space
Furniture
Utilities: electricity, home heating fuel
Storage

Technological Systems and Support

The most variable budgets are those for data processing and
telecommunications. How a telecommuter divides tasks between
office and home determines whether the telecommuting environment—at the high end—fully replicates the office environment in
information processing and transmission capabilities, or whether it
is less sophisticated technologically, able to accommodate only certain tasks. This range also influences start-up costs of telecommuting. There is considerable discretion in how office technology is
replicated in the home.

Organizations can reduce telecommuting equipment costs by:

• leasing or purchasing laptop computers and other equipment for
  shared use
• effective technological training that reduces the need for ongoing technical support;
• group purchasing (facilitated by aggregating telecommuting
  needs of different departments): the Los Angeles County
  telecommuting program secured 30 percent discounts on computing equipment purchased by employees from a number of
  competing vendors.

However, no matter how simply or completely home office equipment echoes machinery used in the office the factor of distance intrudes; it makes itself felt in new telecommunication costs. Telecommunication expenditures cover equipment, usage-sensitive costs such as telephone tolls, communication channels such as telephone lines, and value-added services such as voice mail.

Managers who watch their telephone bills carefully are surprised by the rapidly with which bills jump because of telecommuters calling in from remote work sites. An office buys local measured service and long distance telephone service at the lowest possible rates. A call into an office from a residence can cost five to ten times more than a call out from the facilities of a large organization. In addition, if a telecommuter uses a credit card, he pays a per call surcharge; if he turns in telephone bills for reimbursement, there is overhead to processing and paying the reimbursement.[11] All of these factors conspire against unrestricted telecommunication access for the telecommuter. Depending on a department's budget to underwrite telecommuting, the telecommuter (while off-site) may be constrained from performing certain kinds of work.

Some organizations have less capacity on the office side for inbound communications from telecommuters than they would like. Adding new modem lines and other telephone-based communication services increases technology overhead. Access to office-bound computing systems may require specialized equipment and/or software that is different from the office configuration. For example, an office may share computing facilities via a local area network, while a telecommuter needs dial-up access. Each communication system in an organization has its characteristic software and hardware. According to the technologies used, there could be further overhead in personnel required to design, install, support, and maintain complicated or custom configurations.

Because variable telecommunication costs are partially metered by distance, time of day, volume, duration, and the types of lines required to support them, telecommunication budgets are quite volatile unless they are carefully managed. If a telecommuter can pass or receive telephone messages at off-peak hours, especially between 11 P.M. and 8 A.M., telecommunication costs are greatly reduced. Telecommuters who are away from the office for short spurts—a day or two—can save money by deferring calls until they return to the office, take them rather than make them, and use off-peak, asynchronous messages such as electronic mail and facsimiles as much as possible. Companies can also reduce inbound charges by installing 800 lines for both e-mail and voice mail services at bulk discounts.

General ways to reduce telecommunications costs include:

- encouraging outbound calling from the organization (a receptionist calls a telecommuter with messages so the telecommuting does not call in for them) since telephone calls originating within an organization are generally less expensive than calls originating elsewhere;
- using voice mail to pass messages rather than conversations, and thereby lessening telephone tolls;
- encouraging flextime among telecommuters to allow them to make calls when toll rates are lower.

Clever management of computer data can also make a difference. For example, if the telecommuter batches files, compresses them so they can be sent more quickly, and transmits them after hours, large volumes of data become much more economical to move from home to office.

Managers should not expect most telecommuters to figure out these technological strategies on their own. An in-house expert on information technology and telecommunications will need to show telecommuters how to save money by suggesting computing and telephone tactics that make communications more efficient.

Allocation Policy

The actual cost of telecommuting to the employer depends in part on cost-allocation policies that divide expenses between the employer and the telecommuter. Some employers cover virtually all costs, while others severely restrict the types of costs they will allow and may also impose ceilings on the expenses they will pay. One employer, for example, limited refunds to employees for business telephone calls from home to a percentage of the total. Another would jawbone a telecommuter when the supervisor felt her telephone bill excessive.

The program should educate managers to the consequences of

different cost-allocation schemes. Equity between telecommuters and nontelecommuters argues that employees should not be burdened with costs they would not have to face were they not telecommuting.[12] In this way, it is asserted, employees do not loose rights or status because they are telecommuting. On the other hand, it is also argued that since both employee and employer benefit from telecommuting, both should share the costs.[13]

Depending on the tasks performed while telecommuting and the personal resources of the telecommuter, the employer/employee split could produce inequitable access to the program. Obviously, some tasks are telephone-intensive, but do not require personal computers. In other circumstances, an employee might already own or be willing to purchase a computer for telecommuting while a colleague cannot afford to do so. Informal programs tend to fudge any clear policy; formal programs, by their nature, oblige more even-handed policy-making.

The fact that employees are often willing to buy equipment in order to telecommute certainly encourages employers to expect that their other employees will do so. If an employer adopts a requirement that telecommuters provide their own equipment, inequitable financial burdens could be reduced by establishing a no-interest or low-interest loan program with a generous payback schedule, a company computer store with liberal discounts, or a cut-rate pricing arrangement with equipment vendors.

By tradition, certain telecommuting expenses are always assigned to the telecommuter. They include home-office space, furniture, and home utility costs. Telecommuters accept these expenses because they are balanced by employee savings in commuting costs such as gasoline, automobile depreciation, tolls, and parking, and by personal expenses such as lunch, clothing and food. For many telecommuters, the convenience of flexible work is a form of indirect compensation.

There are no hard and fast rules or even customs that allocate equipment costs between telecommuters and employers. In a survey of readers of *Modern Office Technology* magazine, 55 percent said their employers paid for home computers used for overtime work, and 14.9 percent said their employers paid for all home equipment.[14] With the rapid decline in computer pricing, more and more employees at all income levels are buying machines for their homes and they often make a point of acquiring equipment compatible with what they use in the office.

Cost-allocation could be used to encourage trip-reduction.[15] The greater the trip-reduction resulting from telecommuting, in this scheme, the greater the reimbursement level. This could be combined with a ceiling on expenditures or a maximum reimbursement for total trip-reduction. However, such an arrangement is still conjectural. In America, on the contrary, companies with active commute-reduction programs prefer to discourage commuting by charging commuters to park or by subsidizing alternative transportation modes such as mass transit or vanpooling. These practices encourage telecommuting by cost-avoidance rather than by cost-allocation.

Offsets to Expenditures

Some employers have concluded that the cost benefits of telecommuting are great enough to warrant significant cost coverage. For example, the state of California projects the benefit to cost ratio of telecommuting could reach as high as seven to one. These benefits are returned in reduced sick leave, increased productivity, and improved recruitment and retention of skilled employees.[16,17] Telecommuting consulting firm JALA Associates claims that many of its corporate clients keep such favorable calculations to themselves; they consider the telecommuting programs to be competitive advantages not to be disclosed.

Although some describe the benefits of telecommuting as very tangible, they are not nearly as tangible as increased expenditures. In order for productivity to become a major incentive for flexible work, a clear managerial mandate is essential. Special citations for departments taking flexible work initiatives—perhaps as reflected in a reduction in absenteeism—could encourage their efforts.

As budget constraints force administrative units to make do with less staff, finding ways to increase productivity becomes more of an issue. No administrator wants to fall short of service level goals and face complaints from customers. If management becomes convinced that a fixed staff can meet rising demands for productivity by implementing flexible work, it is more likely to give flexible work a try. This, in turn, may lead to a greater willingness to make outlays for equipment, telecommunications, technological support, and program coordination.

Exposure to Increased Liability

Legal and financial exposure does not, according to all reported experience, increase as a result of flexible work arrangements. No worker's compensation packages include disclaimers or additional fee schedules specific to remote work. Since remote work centers are indistinguishable organizationally from other facilities, they carry identical risks. Work at home appears to be distinguishable, but in fact it is not. The incremental exposure to risk of flexible work is zero except for equipment losses.

Since, however, risk analysis is concerned with displaying what could happen (and implementations that reduce or eliminate the incremental risk), it is necessary to examine the potential for liability evoked by flexible work. There are three areas to consider: worker's compensation, equipment, and discrimination. There are policy and program issues raised by liability concerns; they are discussed at the conclusion of this section.

Worker's Compensation

Worker's compensation in relation to flexible work is not a major issue.[18] The employee's remote work space (whether a home-based office or a work center) is considered, for the purposes of worker's compensation, an extension of the workplace. Consequently, the employee's coverage for job-related accidents is identical to that enjoyed in the central office.[19] However, the home-based telecommuter needs to designate a workspace separate from the rest of the residence. Accidents occurring outside of the designated area would not be covered.

With respect to vehicular accidents, the going and coming rule absolves employers of liability while an employee is commuting. However, if the employee begins work at home and then goes into the office to continue, there is probably coverage since the transit is during work hours for work-related purposes. The same liability would characterize a nontelecommuting employee traveling during work hours to attend a meeting at a distant location.

The one murky area of worker's compensation concerns a temporarily-disabled employee who returns to work as a telecommuter. In a university telecommuting program, a recuperating employee was not permitted to telecommute because the employer determined that a condition worsened by work-at-home (in this case, a medically premature return to work) could expose the university to a claim even though the condition itself was not work-related. Exposure potentials of temporary telecommuting for a recuperating employee should be examined on a case-by-case basis.

In order for a worker's compensation claim to be legitimate, it must be based on injuries received on the job. For a telecommuter, on the job means during the designated times and at the designated places of remote work. Consequently, it is important the telecommuting agreement specify hours of work, and make clear that injuries developed outside of those hours (when, for example, the employee informally flexes work schedule) are not covered; similarly, the work location must be defined as the home office. If a telecommuter suffers a burn in her kitchen preparing a cup of tea, she is not covered, unless the kitchen is her home office and the preparation is job-related. If, however, the agreement specifies flex-time parameters, then workers' compensation coverage will follow.

Coverage for third party injuries sustained as a result of a home-office operated by a telecommuter are not uniformly covered by employer insurance. For example, industrial environments often restrict visitation by nonemployees. In fact, falls and other common office accidents can also occur in a home office; there, flexible work programs should investigate the need for third party coverage, evaluate its costs and value, and determine whether it is needed.[20]

Equipment Losses

The liability for equipment loss follows the employer's policies (both internal and in its insurance) for on-site equipment and equipment loans. These policies should address damage, maintenance and repair, and theft. As recommended earlier, equipment policies should be incorporated into the telecommuting agreement; the employee should know how, for example, water damage to a company's computer is treated if it occurs at a home office. Conversely, employees may bring personally owned equipment to the office (a laptop computer, for example, with data to be transferred to a desktop computer); is it covered?

Employees who purchase their own computers or other equipment for telecommuting should consult an insurance agent about coverage. Standard homeowner and renter insurance policies do not automatically cover equipment in the home used for business purposes; some charge a hefty fee for business equipment riders.[21] Employers would limit their liability by specific exclusions of employee-owned equipment.

Software Duplication

Most companies have learned to protect themselves from exposure through the use of unlicensed software, and software companies have encouraged large organizations to buy site licenses. In small companies, where site licenses may not be economical, telecommuters can generally duplicate a licensed product under the single use rule. This widely understood principle is that a single-user product is legally used if it is not run simultaneously by two or more users, regardless of the number of copies in circulation. Thus, the telecommuter can copy a software product for home use provided that, at any time, usage alternates between the two. If software is licensed for network use by multiple users, home use of the product requires a separate, stand-alone license. User licenses vary from product to product. Caution dictates that companies check with software publishers for pertinent limitations.

Discrimination and Personnel Actions

Gerardine DeSanctis, a popularizer of telecommuting fond of conundrums, counsels that women and minorities might claim telecommuting stints had "adverse impacts" on promotional opportunities in a discrimination suit. In her theory (for no such case has been cited) an employee claims that an employer erected a barrier to promotion by authorizing flexible work. She therefore recommends that the performance of women and minority telecommuters be carefully monitored to avoid a collision between remote work and job advancement.[22]

Part-time telecommuting would seem on its face to obviate this risk. The notion of special monitoring, however, seems even more discriminatory. To the extent that performance is measured by output, an employee would find it difficult to make the case that telecommuting is discriminatory. Employees seeking a promotion should, certainly, be advised in advance if the position sought includes flexible work options, or if it eliminates them.

Flexible work does not by itself increase risk associated with discharge, suspension, or disciplinary action against an employee. However, an employee might argue (in a wrongful termination suit, for example) that a flexible work arrangement was negligent because it encouraged deficient behavior. This is akin to blaming an established starting time for office workers for their tardiness. Still, a department contemplating disciplinary action or termination should cancel flexible work arrangements as a matter of course. There is no gain in making a difficult situation even more complex.

Since flexible work is not an employee prerogative, it is not directly actionable by an employee or by a union, although the consequences of flexible work may be. In terms of actual precedents, the most dangerous shoal confronts employers who are using telecommuting to push employees into independent contractor status. If the employer sells a bill of goods to an employee, as some companies have, adverse consequences to the employee could be litigated.

Policy and Program Considerations

A well-managed flexible work program includes an agreement that explains the responsibilities assumed by both management and staff when flexing time and/or place of work. The agreement should spell out any liabilities, insurance, or risks the flexible worker is expected to assume; it should also include assurances that the flexible worker will not incur any loss of benefits. By the same token, the agreement also specifies that the employer does not assume any new kinds of risks such as damage to the home (except for damage caused by another employee when, for example, installing equipment); plain language explaining risks assumed by the employee is the positive approach.

Home Inspections

There are different views about employer inspections of the home offices of prospective and practicing telecommuters. To minimize risk, the employer would like to determine whether the home-office environment is healthy, safe, and relatively secure from theft or equipment damage.[23,24] Furthermore, one visit is probably not enough to ascertain risks. JALA Associates, the telecommuting consulting firm, recommends home inspections at random times.[25] However, federal flexiplace guidelines for federal government workers observe that

> Occasional visits by the supervisor to the home work site are [an] approved technique, *but can be very intrusive and undermine mutual trust.* . . . If used at all, visits as well as any other monitoring activity should be done in accordance with the written agreement and in a manner that preserves mutual trust and respect. [emphasis added][26]

For many workers, an official visit to the home would be about as welcome as a terrorist attack and a surprise visit good cause for cardiac arrest. Some inspectors may develop unconscious, negative, inappropriate, or subjective attitudes toward an employee or towards the telecommuting option because of observations of a home's condition, of the neighborhood in which it is located, or of an employee's lifestyle.

Instead, employees should certify in flexible work agreements that home offices are safe, healthy, and reasonably secure. Employees should not be compelled to submit a residence to inspection. However, technical personnel, health and safety specialists, a union representative, or a co-worker should be available to help employees organize a home office, and tips about home-office set-up should be included in training sessions. Moreover, the telecommuter agreement also provides that the employer may visit the home office for the limited purpose of retrieving loaner equipment that otherwise might not be returned promptly. Perhaps a telecommuter quits, dies, is terminated, or is too ill to return to work and cannot return company equipment or materials on her own.[27]

Step 6
Establish Flexible Work Policies and Agreements

An organization wisely balances the requirements of a successful program with an evolutionary approach among departments. Micromanagement of departmental operations, no matter what the excuse, is not feasible. What is needed is a relatively short list of company-wide policies and procedures designed to reduce or eliminate problems commonly created by flexible work arrangements.

The short list includes certain general operational policies, the execution of a flexible work agreement, and departmental standards for evaluating the performance of flexible workers. A memorandum of understanding could be signed between the program and a participating department agreeing to the short list, stating what resources the program will make available and when, and naming the flexible work coordinator in the department.

Broad Participation

The most important policy addresses the scale of the program. A policy of broad participation assures that the benefits of flexible work are both garnered throughout the organization and equitably distributed. Even if the number of initial participants is small, the types of participants represented can be broad. As the program unfolds, look closely at the positions, pay scales, and skills of flextime workers and telecommuters. Are they mostly the best paid, most independent professionals and managers, or do clerks, technicians, machine operators, and warehouse men also show up? Part of the function of a program is to alert departments that flexibility benefits now allocated on an occasional, informal basis to a few, chosen employees can be extended to more staff, and maybe even to most.

Nondiscriminatory Performance Standards

The program advances flexible work in part to improve productivity; however, flexible work arrangements should not require participants to meet new performance standards or ones different from those of nonparticipants. In particular, flexible workers should not have to meet onerous standards of accountability for their work. In one instance, an especially anxious manager unfairly required telecommuters to turn in work plans in advance of the days they worked at home, while no itemization was requested of those not telecommuting.

Flexible work arrangements are not in themselves subject to performance evaluation, nor will personnel records reflect participation in them. Of course, other performance standards are unchanged.

The key to getting information needed to appraise flexible workers is an ability to compare expected work with actual work. Both must be known quantities, the one prescriptive, the other retrospective. The process of making expectations clear, and evaluating their realization, is the essence of management by objective (MBO).

The newer MBO is to management, the more effort goes into creating fair conditions for evaluating the performance of flexible workers. Participants can be obliged to submit clear statements of objectives and timelines for their realization, but MBO is not a system of *self* management, but a way of managing an organization; it defines a style among managers, supervisors, flexible workers, and traditional workers alike. Since nearly all, if not all, telecommuting will be part-time, a failure to institute department-wide MBO can end up trivializing the process to the point where their management degenerates into interrogating flexible workers about their accomplishments. Managing flexible workers calls for flexible management. In the beginning of a program, snags in schedules, time lines, and the delilvery of work products are inevitable. These problems, of course, also arise in traditional workplaces, but they can become more visible in the context of flexible work arrangements. Indeed, telecommuting and flextime are easy scapegoats for production problems even in organizations that have always had difficulties coordinating work. The conviction that flexible work is to be blamed is hard to shake.[28]

The antidote is to roll with the punches. If one way of structuring cooperation does not seem to be working—for example, scheduling meetings on short notice—the agile manager will try another. Instead of asking a secretary to chase participants across flextime zones and telecommuting locales, why not designate a specific day when everyone is on site and available for meeting? Says telecommuting consultant David Flemming: "An agency does not have to accept one set pattern. The idea is to let telecommuting work . . ."[29]

Voluntary Participation in Home-Based Telecommuting

Unlike work schedules, telecommuting is almost always an option, not an obligation; departmental management and individuals volunteer to participate in this form of flexible work. The reasons are manifold. Workers may not have the space or social environment that makes working at home practical. Consider the employee whose space is in transition because of divorce, a new home, or rebuilding after a flood. Some employees may accurately judge themselves unable to resist the temptations of food, drink, or drugs away from the workplace; they need the discipline of the traditional environment. While the extent of social isolation among parttime telecommuters is exaggerated, there are those who depend on their workmates to fulfill social needs; these employees would find it hard to concentrate when working alone. Finally, some employees may not be able to afford utility expenses associated with home-based telecommuting such as heating or air conditioning.

From a management perspective, the mutual agreement underlying telecommuting provides an essential escape valve when remote work arrangements are problematic. Perhaps a natural leader of a group has everything in place to telecommute several days a week; after a short time, however, the manager observes that while his performance at home is excellent, members of his work group become rudderless in his absence. Until the manager can resolve this disparity, she may well want the worker back in the workplace. Finally, if an employee can be forced to telecommute, then the argument can be constructed more readily that the employee has a right to telecommute, or that it is in fact a benefit. A large number of employees asserting that right, even if their assertions were individually reasonable, could quickly bring chaos to an organization.

There are exceptions. Remote work centers can be staffed on an involuntary basis because they do not require employees to furnish resources such as space, heat, or electricity normally provided by the employer. Some organizations have required outside sales forces to work from home with mixed results. In the latter case, employers would be well advised to impose the requirement at the point of hire. For example, there are firms that only hire telecommuters; remote work is a condition of employment. In that instance, telecommuting is involuntary.

Involuntary Flextime

Employee schedules, unlike home-based telecommuting, need not be voluntary. Employers generally assert the right to institute starting and ending times of the workday. However, employer-mandated schedules are not considered flextime because the employee's needs for a schedule are not considered. An employee at Hewlett-Packard, for example, is required to start at 5 A.M. so that he is available to his East Coast clients when their day begins at 8 A.M. in their time zone. He doesn't consider himself a flextime worker even although he leaves work at 2 P.M.; he is merely working an unusual shift. Employers should note that involuntary flextime may incur differential pay depending on company policy or an employee's bargaining unit.

Flexible Work, a Mutually-Agreed Arrangement

Flexible work is an option exercised by the mutual agreement of management and worker. Neither can compel the other, in usual circumstances, to implement flexible work. Consequently, a flexible work arrangement is not an employee right or benefit. Management takes into account departmental objectives, employee experience and performance, job description, tool and materials requirements, and team effort in evaluating the eligibility of an employee for flexible work. An employee wishing flexible work arrangements but deemed ineligible should be advised of the reason(s) why.

If, in management's judgment, a flexible work arrangement is proving deleterious to the department or to the performance of an employee, it should be discontinued or amended. The employee should be advised, with notice if at all possible, of the change and the reasons for it. Employees must recognize that from time to time flexible work arrangements may have to be abridged or suspended because of the dynamic nature of an employee's duties or of the department's work or workload.

No flexible work arrangement abridges, qualifies, or otherwise diminishes an employee's rights (including collective bargaining rights), status, benefits, or compensation. Similarly, flexible work arrangements do not alter employee responsibility in matters such as job performance, workload, care and regard for the safety and work of co-workers, or conduct while working.

Affirmative Action

Flexible work arrangements can assist departments in meeting affirmative action goals in the hiring and retention of disabled workers, women, and minorities. However, flexible work should never abrogate integration and advancement of the disabled, women, and minorities in the workplace.

Sensitivity governs how flexible work options are promoted to disadvantaged workers. Special care is taken to avoid any suggestion that, for example, a woman or physically-challenged worker would be more comfortable working off-site. There are two alternatives. First, employees who need flexibility should be given the right to request it; they can make a case based on the nature of their work and its suitability to flextime or telecommuting. Their personal circumstances do not become a management issue.

Second, they may propose flexible arrangements as an alternative to disability or leave. In these special instances, management is legitimately concerned with personal circumstances since the employer may otherwise assume financial liability. Employers do have a right to know the basis, for example, of requests for sick leave or disability. Key to this prescription is that the initiative lies with the employee.

Amending Personnel Policies

The human resources department or comparable body should review personnel policies, including those defined by collective bargaining agreements, to discover whether they conflict with variations in work hours and/or work locations.

For example, a policy may define a shift as 8 A.M. to 5 P.M. In certain compressed work week programs (nine nine-hour days and a day off) shift, work week, and overtime policies need to be changed. Many workers, regardless of coverage by union contracts, are subject to the Federal Labor Standards Act (FLSA). FLSA requires payment of overtime if the work week exceeds forty hours; it has no requirement for overtime payment based on the length of the work day. By defining the start of the shift as noon rather than eight in the morning, a worker can work four nine-hour days plus four hours (36 + 4 = 40 hours in week one), and then four hours plus four nine-hour days (4 + 36 = 40 hours in week two), and achieve one day off every other week without incurring overtime.

One company wanted to establish a bulletin board system (BBS) that could be used by telecommuters and nontelecommuters alike to stay in touch; it had prohibitions, however, against union use of company communication systems. It headed off a potential dispute with a union by exempting the BBS from this prohibition.

Or, depending on the specificity of language, a company may need to change the criteria for differential pay to avoid incrementing pay for staff that starts earlier on a flextime schedule. Or suppose in a compressed work week program that an employee's earned day off coincides with a holiday? The employer needs to make clear how the employee will schedule the extra day off, or, on the contrary, how an hour will be made up if an eight-hour holiday coincides with a nine-hour day? Are there rules about time reporting that need to be adjusted to allow telecommuting days to count? What procedures govern the loan of equipment or the portage of supplies for home use; do they create unusual paperwork for the employee who uses a company computer when telecommuting?

In small professional organizations few polices are codified and alternative work arrangements pose no special policy challenge; informal understandings are adequate. In large, complex organizations with dozens of union contracts, highly developed personnel policies filling thick manuals, and a maze of closely observed state and federal labor laws, conforming flexible work arrangements may be a heady task.

Large organizations can create a bubble of temporary exceptions to personnel policies tied to a prototype, and put off a comprehensive revision to policies (and contracts) until they are certain flexibility is around to stay. Any company with union contracts should be especially alert to "meet and confer" requirements that must precede changes in work hours, reporting times, or work site of covered employees.

The flexible work agreement proposed below functions as an understanding, not a contract, between flexible workers and management. It should not have any effect on company personnel policies. Nonetheless, the prudent company will have legal counsel review standardized flexible work agreements before execution.

A Program That Enables

Successful programs work with rather than against departmental authority; rules, standards, and policies of the program must be handled carefully. Handled well, departments will feel that the program enhances not only employees' flexibility, but their own management and supervisory authority.

Flexible work in all of its varieties is an ongoing, informal practice in many organizations with or without official sanction. Even with a formal policy, informal flexible work arrangements will continue. On the other side, programs work best if departmental management are persuaded rather than goaded. Enabling policies put flexibility forward without pushing anyone's face into it.

Still, the consistency and integrity of the organization's program suggests a carrot to encourage a particular slant to departmental implementations. Departments that implement flexible work in a way that meets certain program standards gain access to certain incentives. No department is obliged to conduct flexible work other than within the boundaries of general personnel policy. Adoption of program policies is purely voluntary. However, program resources (such as training) are made available only to those departments that implement program policies. There is no point to having a confrontation with a department manager over individual deals he has made.

Flexible Work Agreements

All flexible work arrangements should be based on a flexible work agreement signed by management and employee. A model agreement is shown here. The agreement defines how changes in work arrangements are to be handled. It eliminates common ambiguities in flexible work arrangements that cause expectations of management and flexible workers to clash.

A signed agreement (1) assures that management and employee have the same, simultaneous understanding of how the program works, (2) allocates the responsibility for equipment between the employer and the employee, and (3) specifies matters such as hours of work. Because telecommuters, in particular, are not visually monitored as they work, the agreement is the "long arm of policy" extending to the alternative work site.[30]

General operational and program policies should be incorporated into the agreement as standard content. The balance of the agreement consists of departmental and job-specific policies.[31] As the program matures, it will modify policy and practices. Consequently, the agreement should also include language like that used by Pacific Bell: "The following guidelines are evolving and subject to change. . . ."[32]

Some versions of telecommuting agreements extend it to include detailed statements of performance requirements.[33] While jobs may be so static that they can be incorporated, the inclusion of such content misses the point of the agreement. The flexible work agreement spells out flexibility, not the job, job-related duties, or assignments. Consequently, flexible work agreements would be unlikely to contain language typically found in a position description.

This model agreement combines flextime and telecommuting because all of the latter apply to the former. That is, telecommuters usually restructure their hours of work as well as their location of work. In handouts distributed to departments, however, separate model agreements for flextime are needed because, as a rule, most flextime workers do not telecommute.

The flexible work agreement provides a useful place to put a

MODEL FLEXIBLE WORK AGREEMENT

Note: Examples are underlined, comments are in italics.

(A) Departmental Flexible Work Coordinator

Name:_____

Telephone Number:_____

(B) Official Duty Station

For the purpose of this agreement, your official duty station is: _____

For most employees, the official duty station is the office; there may be field workers, however, whose duty station is a home, satellite work center, facilities of another department, etc.

(C) Leaves of Absence or Changes in Position

> Continuation of flexible work arrangements are not assured if an employee takes a protracted leave of absence or changes or transfers positions.

(D) Hours of Work

The hours of work are from <u>8:00 a.m. until 5:00 p.m.</u>

> The employee will maintain a record of hours worked and locations of work.

>The employee will maintain, for the purposes of Worker's Compensation liability, the hours of work stated in this Agreement.

> When they are in conflict, departmental requirements take precedence over the schedule and telecommuting arrangements specified in this Agreement. Management will provide the employee with advance notice if at all possible when flextime schedules or telecommuting must be curtailed.

> During days of partial telecommuting, commute hours between home and company facilities will count as hours worked according to company policy.

> Differential pay will be applied only when the agreed schedule, departing from the standard shift, is required for the performance of work; differential pay may be denied if a telecommuter shifts the work period to a time for which differential is not available.[40]

> Compensatory time-off, CTO accumulation, leave-without-pay, vacation time, and/or overtime must be authorized according to company policy.

(E) Flextime Schedule

The employee will begin work at <u>7:00 a.m.</u> and conclude work at <u>4:00 p.m.</u>
The flextime schedule may be modified at the employee's discretion.

The agreement here spells out the bandwidth of flextime, any core hour requirements, options for flexible scheduling of the lunch hour, and any other options the company makes available.[41]

> Downtime of two hours or less occasioned by equipment problems, household emergencies, etc., may be shifted within the same day at the employee's convenience; downtime of four hours or more must be reported within <u>two hours</u> to the employee's supervisor for make-up, Leave Without Pay, or Compensatory Time Off. Downtime is time when a telecommuter is unable to work.

> The established working hours of the Department begin at <u>8:00 a.m.</u> and end at <u>5:00 p.m.</u> Technical, supervisory, or collegial support cannot be assured at other times. Downtime experienced outside of established working hours because of unavailable support must be made up by the employee.[42]

(F) Insurance

> A designated work space shall be maintained by the telecommuter at the alternate work location. Worker's compensation liability will be limited to this work space as opposed to applying to all areas of the home.

A risk manager should evaluate whether third parties injured in the home work space are covered or should be covered; this issue developed, as mentioned, in a SEIU critique of the County of Los Angeles telecommuting program. In general, Worker's Compensation for work-related injury is unaffected by the location of the environment in which the injury occurs.

(G) Health and Safety

> The employee is expected to maintain the same standards of health and safety whether telecommuting or working in the employer's facility.

> Employees are urged to seek the assistance of health and safety specialists, of this Department's management, or of coworkers in advising, establishing, and/or evaluating the health and safety of the home office environment.

Telecommuters must either sign the following certification or agree to a health and safety inspection of their home offices.

Certification: I, <u>employee name</u>, certify that my home office used for telecommuting meets reasonable health and safety standards, including standards for ergonomic computing, and I release the company from any liability for compromise of my health or safety resulting from my home office for telecommuting.

(Employee Signature)
(Date)

Makeshift home offices may not be appropriately designed to protect an employee from repetitive motion injuries. Given the eventuality of federal regulatory standards for "ergonomic computing," an employer may want to incorporate ergonomic guidelines into the agreement. This could take the form, for example, of a chart specifying the physical arrangement of keyboard, computer monitor, and seating.

(H) Training

> Participation in the official flexible work training program made available through this department and the flexible work program is mandatory unless a written exemption is obtained from the Department's Flexible Work Coordinator.

(I) Equipment

> Personal use of company equipment made available for telecommuting is permitted as long as your personal use of the equipment contributes to your proficiency with it, does not harm it, and does not conflict with other company rules and regulations. You may not use company equipment for unlawful purposes or for work for other employees, nor may other persons use it.[43]

> Any hardware or software purchased by the company remains the property of the company and will be returned to the company on request; products developed while telecommuting are the property of the company.

> Department will purchase <u>laptop computers</u> for loan to telecommuters on a per use basis (i.e., computers are not to remain in the remote office when the employee is at the department) OR for a specific period of time, namely, <u>from September 1, 1996 through September 1, 1997</u> OR for use until recalled by the company.

> The attached inventory must be signed prior to the removal of company equipment from company premises.

> Equipment loan forms shall be used when removing equipment from the office for telecommuting purposes.

> Department will not provide <u>answering machines, facsimiles, or photocopiers</u> for home use.

Sometimes a department will specify that it does not make furniture or answering machines available to telecommuters.

> Telecommuters are prohibited <u>from calling the company collect except in case of emergency.</u>

> Equipment provided by the Department will be maintained by the Department. The Department is not responsible for the temporary loss of telecommuting days due to equipment maintenance or repair and the employee is expected to report to the office or obtain approved leave in such a circumstance.

> Equipment no longer used by a telecommuter must be returned on his or her next day in the office.

> Employee may, at their option, have a company technician assist with the installation of technical equipment in their home-office.

> Software used by telecommuters is subject to the same company restrictions on duplication and unauthorized use as software used in the office.

> The company assumes no responsibility for the repair, maintenance, or replacement of personally-owned equipment used for telecommuting.

(J) Visits

> Visits to employee home offices will be made only if authorized by the employee for health and safety inspection or to retrieve company equipment which the employee has not returned after being requested to do so.

(K) Security of Information

> Employees may not compromise the confidentiality or security of company infomation due to telecommuting, remote computer access, etc. Unauthorized disclosure, perusal, or altering of information by an employee is an extremely serious violation of company policy. Breeches of information security whether by accident or design while telecommuting may be cause to abrogate the option and/or for disciplinary action.

(L) Reimbursements and Telecommuting Expenses

> Work-related telecommunication costs associated with telecommuting will be reimbursed.

> Telecommuter must obtain supplies stocked at the department from the department and will not be reimbursed if they are obtained elsewhere.

> Expenses not specifically covered above will be dealt with on a case by case basis, taking into account the reasonableness of the expense, other expenses reimbursed for the same employee or to other employees performing similar duties, and the overall budget for the program. The employee cannot be assured of reimbursements for expenses not approved in advance.

> Your supervisor, <u>Beth Anderson</u>, will have authority to review, approve or disallow reimbursement requests not specifically covered above.

(M) Domestic Care

> Flexible work is not a replacement for domestic care responsibilities. During established work hours, the telecommuter agrees that care demands shall not compete with work except in the case of an emergency (see Hours of Work, above).

(N) Length of Telecommuting Period

Telecommuters shall telecommute for a maximum of <u>two</u> years without written reauthorization.

Some proponents of telecommuting suggest an upper limit of two years since, they argue, skills and office relations will wither. Depending on the job, the frequency of telecommuting, and the office, this might not be so. Departments should evaluate the length of a telecommuter arrangement. Some need not have a fixed maximum. These will include arrangements about which a manager is not fully convinced.

(O) Tax liability

> The tax implications of telecommuting are entirely the responsibility of the telecommuter. Telecommuters are encouraged to seek professional advice in this area.

Indeed, telecommuters receive few if any tax breaks as regular, full-time employees working at home.[44,45,46] Whether telecommuters save any money is questionable when savings in food, commuting, and clothing are balanced with increased costs in heating, equipment, furniture, and space.

(P) Local Zoning Ordinances

> The telecommuter is responsible for observing any municipal zoning ordinances regulating the performance of work at home for telecommuting purposes.

This issue is raised but never documented in popular articles on telecommuting. On the contrary, many local governments are encouraging telecommuting as a form of job-creation. Local regulations regarding home-based businesses have no conceivable impact on telecommuting unless the telecommuter generates traffic receiving business visitors at the home-office.

(Q) Cooperation with Evaluation and Research

> Employees participating in flextime and/or telecommuting programs are expected to cooperate with evaluation and research projects authorized by management. Participants with questions regarding research, evaluation, data collection, or the confidentiality of information provided for research purposes should contact the department's flexible work coordinator.

Signature and date (employee)_____

Signature and date (supervisor or manager)_____

checklist of actions the flextime worker or telecommuter should take before the alternative work arrangements begin. It should probably be used as the conspicuous cover sheet of the agreement. The checklist might enumerate, for example, the following:[41]

❑ Employee has read flexible work policies and procedures.
❑ Schedules for telecommuting and/or flextime are established.
❑ Equipment issued to telecommuter is documented.
❑ Performance expectations are clearly understood.
❑ Employee attended training sessions as required.
❑ Home-office requirements have been reviewed with employee.
❑ Employee home-office telephone number:_____.
❑ Employee has signed Flexible Work Agreement.
❑ Employee has signed certification of home-office safety and security.

Step 7
Secure Management and Employee Commitment

M anagers and employees are brought into a flexible work pro- gram in four steps. Depending upon the size, culture, and structure of an organization, it may divide each step into two sub- steps, one for managers and supervisors, one for nonsupervisory personnel. The former often have questions and concerns that they do not wish to raise in front of those they manage; so, for example, the company will then call orientation meetings limited to manage- ment and meetings open to all.

Whether your organization comes to flexible work through em- ployee discussions or executive foresight, the single most important factor of success is management resolve. Even well-designed flexi- ble work programs flounder when authorized but not advocated by their institution's leadership.[42] Like a vibrating bridge, they get torn apart by indecision over which way to bend. In this way, a flexible work program compares to any significant organizational change.

Unless the executive level campaigns for acceptance of flexibility among middle managers and line supervisors, the program will likely crash and burn. Middle managers and supervisors, apt to see all of the risks but none of the rewards, will resist until the project collapses. Departmental directors, chief administrators, middle managers, and supervisors must be motivated, then mobilized for flexible work.

Here's how the CEO of the Southern California Association of Governments expressed a mandate for flexible work:

... Management strongly supports this experiment, and hopes to see a successful outcome. We recognize that some adjustments to our usual way of doing things will be necessary in order for this to occur. We urge all staff to be flexible and cooperative during this period of adjustment. . . . I urge all of you to be open minded about changing the "accepted" way of doing things, and to expend every reasonable effort to make this project a success.[43]

The management commitment to change needs to reverberate throughout the organization. In smaller organizations, executives should meet directly with subordinates and employees to explain flexibility goals and the reasons for them. In medium-size organizations, an open letter to the staff can explain the rationale for flexible work, the organization's commitment to it, and the way the program will develop. In large organizations, a short videotape featuring the CEO, the head of human resources, and perhaps other divisional leaders is effective and inexpensive to produce. The enthusiastic quality of the executive commitment is the key message to get across in whatever media are used.

An elaborate rationale is not necessary. A simple statement that might identify some or all of the following reasons for flexibility will suffice:

- Increasing productivity
- Improving morale and job satisfaction
- Reducing commuter congestion and stress
- Reducing conflicts with family life and care-giving
- Improving use of office space
- Increasing the value of information technology

Educating the Workforce

The company must explain to the workforce what it is trying to accomplish with flexibility. This is accomplished by the distribution of reading materials, open forums, guest lecturers, and perhaps distribution of videocassettes. An organization fortunate enough to have a library may want to organize a shelf of materials on flexible work that includes books, brochures, and articles from magazines and management journals.

Develop and Distribute Educational Materials

The program will need to develop, publish and reprint, and widely distribute promotional and educational materials. The content of printed materials can draw heavily on existing publications in the public domain while including original material. Small organizations may find employee handbooks and comprehensive personnel policies beyond their means to assemble. They will rely more on already published material. Even then, however, a two- or three-page memorandum from the organization on flexible work is essential; workers need to know what their own employer intends to accomplish; it does not help for their expectations and understandings to be fashioned only by outsiders. Larger organizations, accustomed to the preparation of employment literature, will develop suitable materials for flexible work.

Written materials need not be costly to distribute. Energy departments in state governments, local transportation agencies, telephone companies, and other advocates of flexible work often provide bulk quantities of literature about flextime and telecommuting free to requesting organizations. A number of state and local governments have produced handbooks without copyright protection, designed for adaptation by organizations wishing to use them.[44] Before warming up the photocopier, the flexible work coordinator should make a round of calls to see what's available.

Any of the following types of promotional material are commonly used during the life of the prototype:

- A general brochure or memorandum describing and motivating the program
- Posters for employee bulletin boards
- A newsletter highlighting issues and experiences
- Educational brochures about flextime and telecommuting
- A workbook on flexible work written for department management
- A general guide to relevant technology
- Selected reprints from magazines and books
- Sample applications and agreements
- Policy guidelines
- Self-guided tutorial on using the BBS (if a BBS is established)
- Evaluation surveys and interviews
- Evaluation report

Once the promotional and educational components are agreed on by the program's managers, a budget for material preparation and printing can be put in place.

Promote Program to Departmental Managers

Early adopters, managers who volunteer to participate in flexible work prototypes from the beginning, are a self-selecting group. They're willing to take risks with upside potential. They may be more disposed to managing by objective rather than managing visually. In part, then, the first task of the flexible work program is to find willing managers.

Self-selection may not, however, produce the diversity of participation able to demonstrate benefits of flexible work to the organization as a whole. Not surprisingly, for example, there may be a solid response from the information systems group but hardly a word from the secretarial pool. To achieve a broad spectrum of flexible work arrangements requires active promotion and recruitment by the flexibility planning team. Management and supervisorial groups should be targeted based on the kinds of positions they manage. Uncooperative managers, certainly, will do a program no good, but there always those on the fence. They will give flexibility a try if they believe they'll get recognition and support and protection in the event of failure.

Once departments have signed onto the flexibility program, the coordinator should invite those departments to interesting, short, and informative "dog and pony shows." A video of top executives—or even a simple cassette recording of their statements—provides a strong, attention-grabbing opening to the staff program. The rest of the program should cover the company's rationale for flexibility, its view of flextime, telecommuting, and remote work, the kind of prototype it envisions, the importance of department-level support, and the organizational process that will be used to implement the prototype.

Develop Cooperative Agreements with Departments

The departmental commitment is established when a department signs a memorandum of understanding with management. This memorandum functions like a flexible work agreement, and defines expectations between the program and the department. The program commits to providing resources, as discussed, while the department agrees to implementing program policies, cooperating with research and evaluation, and striving for success (defined, for example, as a certain percentage of participation).

Most organizations are unaccustomed to signing agreements with themselves. However, internal commitments are important milestones in organizational change; they harmonize thinking with doing, and add momentum to the change effort. The memorandum of understanding should not be complicated or appear full of "fine print." It might read like the example shown here.

An employee's success with flexible work depends on a positive approach by his supervisors and managers. There are no successful end-runs of departments in alternative work arrangements. Even if a program coordinator could sign up employees directly for flexible work, the arrangements would quickly fail without the support of departments. Executing a memorandum of understanding emphasizes this support.

Promote Program to Departmental Staff

Individual departmental meetings should be held as widely as possible, although a company might want a general, company-wide forum to kick-off the program. It is probably more efficient but certainly less effective to invite clusters of departments to briefings. Meetings with departments might be prioritized according to estimates of flexible work potential.

Identify Interested Staff

The program should encourage rather than discourage expressions of interest from employees. Although it is human nature to prefer to avoid creating situations were the "big NO" may be necessary, employees know their jobs very well. Often, they have surprisingly good ideas about how they might use flexibility. Only by broadly soliciting applications will these ideas get attention.

Interested employees should apply by completing a question-

ABC Company
Memorandum of Understanding
Flexible Work Program

The _____ Department agrees to participate in the forthcoming
prototype of flexible work arrangements. We will assign _____ as
our Departmental Coordinator and _____ as the department's
manager responsible for flexible work arrangements.

We will be responsible for selecting interested employees for flextime and/or
telecommuting arrangements. Those selected as well as others in their work groups
will receive training from the program; we will be responsible for technological
support. We will cooperate the program evaluation and research projects authorized by the company. We will endeavor to implement all flexible work policies
and procedures of the company, and to encourage all suitable positions to utilize
flexibility when appropriate.

We understand that flexible work arrangements are mutually-agreed options
between employees and managers and may be withdrawn if, in the opinion of
management, they are proving harmful to the work of the department. We also
understand that performance evaluations and promotional opportunities are not
qualified by an employee's interest in or selection for alternative work arrangements.

We have identified the following positions (type, number) as candidates for
flexible work arrangements (type) out of (number) positions held:

Position Description Number Held Number/Flexible Arrangements

Signed and dated [Department Management]
Signed and dated [Program Coordinator]

---

naire explaining how the employee's position is suited to flextime
or telecommuting, proposing types of flexible arrangements, a
schedule, and the work the employee proposes to perform during
alternative schedules and/or locations.

A questionnaire might ask the following:

- What flexible work arrangement(s) are you requesting? Be specific as to starting time, ending time, midday flexibility, and telecommuting location.
- What duties of yours will be affected and how?
- Why are they suited to flexible work arrangements?
- Identify the types of tasks you will perform during alternative work hours and/or job location.
- What impact do you expect your flexible arrangements will have on co-workers (be specific)?
- What technology requirements would you have (such as telephone linkages, computers, etc.) for flextime and/or telecommuting? What contributions, if any could you make to meeting such requirements?
  For example, do you have a personal computer suited to work? Would you need another telephone line installed or could you use one already installed?
- What experience with flexible work arrangements have you had, if any?
- What advantages and disadvantages do you foresee with alternative work arrangements?

Even if a participant satisfactorily answers the questions posed by the application, there may be sound management reasons for disallowing flexibility because of the position, because of the person filling it, or because of technical barriers. However, the proposed process establishes a positive momentum to processing requests.

Some proponents suggest asking employees why they want flexibility, a condescending question likely to get back irrelevant justifications even while it raises privacy issues. Participants, instead, should make essentially the management case, one that addresses the good of the organization. This is more useful because it shows how the employee will help maintain production and manage his or her team responsibilities. This approach is mandatory in the case of disabled employees. As a matter of federal law, asking an employee to talk about her disability is discriminatory unless the employer is requested to finance leave time.

Once departments (and managers and supervisors) and participants have been identified, and their arrangements are locked down, training begins.

Step 8
Train Managers, Supervisors, and Employees

Quality training of flexible workers and managers is essential preparation for the changes the organization will soon experience. Like the flexible work agreement, training is a tool for anticipating and resolving issues before they become problems. Among the programmatic variables of importance, training is second in significance only to the leadership's mandate for change. It establishes common ground between supervisors and participants, provides tips and tactics for participants, gives major policies momentum, and simplifies program administration by providing forums where paperwork, introductions, and other nuts and bolts can be completed.

Since the issues they confront differ, distinct training sessions are held for (1) managers and supervisors, (2) participants, and (3) nonparticipants. Then a session should bring all three groups together.[45] If the sessions work, they create the vigorous climate of communication so essential to the long-term viability of the flexible work program. "We . . . spend a lot of time [in training sessions] creating the right environment," explains a Traveler's spokesman.[46]

The common sessions, where managers, participants, and nonparticipants meet, are the most intense.[47] They focus less on serene information than on frank, open discussion of doubts, anxieties, and potential sources of conflict between management and participants. They provide a forum where expectations are synchronized, an approach taken by U.S. West, a telephone company:

186

Supervisors, prospective telecommuters and in-office staff receive a day of training where each party asks the others, 'what do you expect of me?' and tells 'what I expect of you.'[48]

Depending on the number of participants, format, and the complexity of flexible work options, sessions can run from a few hours to a full day. Some companies reinforce classroom-style sessions with private sessions of the supervisor, the participant, and the co-ordinator. Unless, however, the numbers of participants are very, very small, these sessions would be convened only after implementation, and then to mend rocky relations between a supervisor and a participant.

Elements of management training can include:

Adapting to change[49]
Appraising the performance of remote workers[50]
Effect of flexible work on departmental work flow
Effective communications with flextime workers and telecommuters
Effects of flexible work schedules on co-workers
How to evaluate departmental experiences
How to evaluate productivity changes
Flexible work agreements
Flexible work policies
Handling research and evaluation data
Keeping telecommuters linked to the office[51]
Managing by objective
Planning around schedules and availability
Project management
Prototyping flexible work arrangements
Technical support
Useful technologies
Troubleshooting

Elements of participant training, in alphabetical order, can include:

Adapting to change
Cabin fever (extended telecommuting)
Communication with co-workers
Cooperation with evaluation and research

Coordinating office work and home work
Effective family relations while telecommuting
Flexible work agreements
How telecommuters dress
Maintaining good relationships with supervisors
Managing domestic responsibilities when telecommuting
Managing information resources from home
Organizing job objectives
Personal safety during flextime schedules
Scheduling meetings
Setting up the home office
Technical installations
Technical support
Time management
Useful technologies

Communications

Communications, as opposed to telecommunications, is the essence of successful management—with or without flexible work arrangements. However, experiences in telecommuting programs show that the manager assumes an extra responsibility to perfect his or her communication with staff. They are less visible because of shifting schedules or flexiplace arrangements. Rosemary Guiley explains:

> Since managers of remote employees miss the advantage of eye contact and body language, they must learn to be very specific in verbal communication. Being a good listener is vital. . . . And, says one telecommuter, "managers must have the skill to provide honest and timely feedback."[52]

In many instances, the manager becomes the linker between co-workers, facilitating and even officiating over intraoffice communications.[53] Tom Miller, an oft-quoted source of business research on telecommuting, reminds the manager that "It's easy to become paranoid when you're out of touch with the workplace."[54] Thus, even though telecommuters appreciate flexible arrangements, they remain reliant on management for reassurance that their contributions to the organization count.

Training Nonparticipants

Nonparticipants, sometimes the orphaned majority in flexible work programs, play important roles in making flexible work successful, and their training should not be neglected. It is not uncommon, for example, for telecommuters to face resentment from those remaining in the office. In one organization, a telecommuter was always asked greeted on return by a co-worker, "Well, how was your day off?" The telecommuter became quite resentful, and the work atmosphere suffered. In more extreme cases, nonparticipants may not cooperate with participants on work matters.

A straight-up approach, in advance, can help nonparticipants accept the responsibility they have for flexible work arrangements. They need to understand what telecommuting and flextime are about, why they are important to the organization as well as to participants, and how work groups need to pull together even as the workers in them are partially separated by differing schedules and worksites. Thus, most of the training elements of participant sessions carry over to those of nonparticipant sessions. Creating a positive, supportive atmosphere among co-workers, where both participants and nonparticipants respect one another's work arrangements, is necessary.

Nonparticipants need to be oriented to the changes in the way the office runs. For example, secretaries need to understand that when an individual is working at home, it is perfectly correct to contact that individual and, as a rule, to give out a home-office telephone number (or use the office call-forwarding system), something traditionally never done.

Flextime

Training for flextime workers is simpler than it is for telecommuters; none of the technical aspects of remote work are present. Still, communications and coordination issues obvious in telecommuting also arise in flextime since schedule overlap may be as much as halved. Effective communication among flextime workers, supervisors, and co-workers becomes more demanding, relies more on messages via paper, e-mail, and voice mail, and on better organized communication during common hours. Be aware and beware of the busybody who spends more time worrying about someone else's schedule than his own. Before the well is poisoned, pull that person aside for a talk.

Training Contracts

Perhaps the best niche for consultants (if they are not brought in to run the program) is training. Experienced consultants have training strategies ready to go. Their fees compete favorably with the costs of starting in-house training from scratch. For a company new to flexible work, consultants are a treasure trove of instructive anecdotes and antidotes to reinventing the wheel. In many cities, telecommuting advisory committees (TACs) have been organized, often consisting of institutional representatives and academics. On occasion, professors active in TACs will be willing and accomplished trainers and consultants.

If a company has skill developing training programs, of course, it may prefer to put together its own sessions and borrow information from books, articles, and telephone interviews with telecommuters and flextime workers in other organizations. Still, what managers and participants on the eve of implementation need are not abstractions or exhortations, but concrete advice. In-house trainers could arrange to sit in on training sessions run by an institution experienced in flexible work to get a nitty-gritty sense of the questions asked.

Aside from information, trainees bring fixed ideas, often negative, to the party; thus, part of the training task is to open minds, challenge misunderstandings and misgivings, and move the audience as much as possible to a positive consensus. Meeting planners must therefore schedule ample time for questions and discussions.

Technology Training

Technology training presents a unique challenge. It is impossible to standardize telecommuting technology, to say to telecommuters and their departments, "This is what you need, here's what it costs, and this is how you get it." Unfortunately, that's what much of the flexible work press attempts. Here's what the *Wall Street Journal*, for example, says the telecommuter should have:

A personal computer, a letter-quality printer, an answering machine, a facsimile machine, a two-line telephone, modem, productivity software, telecommunications software, two telephone lines, e-mail service.

In fact, some telecommuters need much more, as any graphic artist who telecommutes would testify—and some telecommuters do well with much less. A book editor readily telecommutes with nothing more than a telephone, pencils, a pile of manuscripts—and a pencil sharpener. Technological tools and materials used in the office are the reliable guides to those useful in a home office. If, as is likely, there are wide disparities among departments and even within departments in the technologies they use, how can a trainer hope to cover all bases?

Furthermore, if the program involves a large number of telecommuters, their numbers can become as much of a training problem as the variety in the technologies they use. People like individual instruction in technology so they can ask questions without embarrassment; what is obvious to one computer user can be completely inscrutable to another. Even if a group of telecommuters were using identical systems, teaching them as a group could be very hard.

To overcome these obstacles, training remote workers in technology should generally be decentralized as much as possible to departments and even to work groups within departments. For a given level of technology, a department generally acquires a corresponding level of expertise to handle day-to-day operations. There is almost always at least one person in the department who understands what a telecommuting co-worker needs in the home office and who can help put it together. Perhaps some departments cannot help themselves in this way; at least, however, the burden on the program to provide technology-specific training will become more manageable.

There are some generic aspects to the extension of office technology to remote sites that can be taught en masse to telecommuters throughout an organization:[55]

Access to departmental LANs
Computer and telephone technologies for the physically disabled
Computer security
Computer to computer communication
Document and data exchange between dissimilar systems

Facsimile access
Laptop technology
Off-site electronic mail
Photocopying
Printing in the home environment
Remote dictation
Teleconferencing
Telephone costs
Telephone service
Voice messaging

In a brief tour of these subjects, telecommuters can become more aware of the kinds of technologies they might employ. They can use such a list to help organize more specific discussions with departmental experts or other technologists who may be available.

Unfortunately, departments that have poorly trained users, inadequate technology management resources, or expect technology to work like magic will not easily support remote technology. If the habit of working with on-site staff to develop technological literacy isn't there, the training channels won't suddenly emerge because of telecommuting. In this circumstance, flexible workers may even need to find support outside of the company.

A number of new services have starting providing twenty-four-hour telephone support for popular software packages; they can be accessible for a per-use fee, on contract for a group of workers, and even via 900 "information services." Many of their customers are small organizations and departments, but they will increasingly serve telecommuters and home-based businesses. Admittedly, outsiders are unlikely to provide the level of specificity that telecommuters need when interacting with complex office systems.[56] However, if the hardware a telecommuter needs can be assembled correctly, software problems can usually be resolved over the telephone. Indeed, some firms have the telecommuter set up and use hardware in the office first, where technical support is available, so that there is less confusion when the telecommuter reassembles the equipment at home.

Electronic Bulletin Board Services

Consider the establishment of an electronic bulletin board service (BBS) to provide ongoing training and improve company communications overall. A bulletin board, among other applications, would certainly include an ask the experts section about telecommuting technology. BBS technology is particularly well suited to answering questions because the expert and the questioner need not schedule a meeting or telephone conversation; experts that one could grow old waiting to reach on the telephone can be quickly contacted through a bulletin board.

The initial users of the BBS will be technicians, computer specialists, and technologists interested in the process as much as the content; as time passes, more and more telecommuters and flextime workers as well as nonparticipants will log on to see what their co-workers have to say.[57] A bulletin board can be easily integrated in a local area network or LAN. There is basic but functional bulletin board software available for free (as shareware) or at low cost; adequate BBSs can be installed on older, otherwise obsolete computers. All in all, a BBS is a simple, low-cost training and communication system.

Step 9
Resolve Problems As they Arise

S tatus checks on the flexible work prototype throughout its life is essential. The most effective check is a series of meetings with managers, supervisors, participants, and nonparticipants. Departments with more than a few flexible workers (more than 10) may consider organizing focus groups and/or support groups.

The experience of many established flexible work program shows the value of having focus groups meet after the first several months of flexible work arrangements. It may be critical to success in some departments. As a rule, focus groups bring together work groups to compare perspectives and issues. However, in programs having problems, sometimes separate focus groups (for managers, participants, and nonparticipants) are organized. Since these discussions are not now speculative, as they were during the planning stage, some feelings may be charged and negative. A group facilitator trusted on all sides and working separately with them, perhaps an outside consultant, might be most effective in taking the pulse of the program and resolving difficulties. They should include nonparticipants to ferret out problems with coordination and cohesion. The goal of the focus groups are to give everyone a chance to identify problems forthrightly and to encourage managers and staff to work together to solve them. Talking issues through increases cooperation and strengthens programs significantly.

The support group is a less result-driven version of the focus group. It is sometimes promoted as a way to reduce telecommuter isolation; however, isolation can be best remedied by part-time arrangements. Rather, support groups provide comfortable, informal arenas for sharing ideas, experiences, and solutions. Support groups can be convened in person—or even electronically.

Step 10
Evaluate Results

A thorough, competent evaluation of the prototype is a lens through which an organization sees the future of flexibility. It is also the fulcrum for decisions that will shape that future. IBM Canada parleyed the prototypical experience of twenty-nine staffers in Ottawa to a commitment to having 15 percent of its marketing representatives telecommute, some 700 workers. They extrapolated a million dollars a year in office space savings at this level of participation.[58] Even a very modestly sized prototype can set profound changes in motion; the evaluation becomes a strategic event.

Given its importance, organizations may be willing to pay for a formal evaluation of a flexible work prototype, even to the point of engaging an independent professional to conduct it. A formal evaluation returns better information, and an independent evaluator may elicit more frank responses in surveys and interviews.

The evaluation asks diverse actors—managers, supervisors, participating and nonparticipating employees, even customers—a common set of questions fair to the effort and connected to the initial goals of the program. An evaluation should reveal, for example, whether:

- Targets were met in numbers, diversity, and productivity
- There were different outcomes to flextime and telecommuting
- There were situations that plainly failed

- Some goals were unrealistic and set expectations too high
- The predicted level of buy-in quite differed from the actual level
- Technological problems hindered and helped flexible arrangements
- Benefit exceeded cost
- Training was effective
- Customer service was affected

The evaluation, as well, must be open to twists and turns of the program, to both positive outcomes and problems utterly unanticipated at the prototype's beginning.

Although the evaluation follows the period of the prototype, it should be thought through at the beginning; otherwise, valuable data may be lost. For example, the evaluator will want logs of training sessions to see who participated. There may be before and after interviews to measure changes in management and employee attitudes. For example, a supervisor may sit on his hands at the beginning of the prototype, skeptical or even hostile, and then experience a change of view months later after hearing about successes in other departments.

Partnerships with Academia

Despite two decades of promotion, study, and experience, flexible work continues to attract scholarly interest, and state and federal grants continue to be available to academic researchers to pursue those interests. Academic research can provide the data needed to evaluate programs.[59,60] A company willing to become a test bed may therefore be able to form a partnership with an academic team, enjoy the fruits of this team's labor at no direct cost, and advance research.

The value of research can be enhanced by making sure that key questions of management are incorporated into the research plan. For example, a researcher interested in commuting might not ask questions about productivity unless specifically asked to do so. Program leadership should work closely with researchers to establish research goals.

The program and participating departments will need to guarantee evaluator access. This includes the distribution and return of questionnaires, efficient scheduling of interviews, and access to personnel and payroll data. Evaluators need to know that they won't be encumbered by reluctant respondents or a hesitant personnel director.

If cooperation with researchers is a new experience, the staff time they will need may not be appreciated. Some organizations have had problems getting employees to fulfill research requirements once a project gets underway. Researchers usually plan data gathering activities carefully to minimize intrusions on the workday and to protect the privacy of individuals. An organization will want research defined in specific terms (e.g., three surveys that will take about a hour each to complete), and to make sure that flexible workers and nonparticipating, control groups are fully prepared to cooperate.

Personal data is essential to many kinds of evaluations. Employees should receive written assurances about how confidential, personal data will be safeguarded, and what data will be summarized in presentations to management. For example, researchers are usually interested in the impact of flexible work on family life. How should information about home life become part of the datastream of a flexible work program evaluation? A number of selection questionnaires now in circulation ask for information that employers do not have a legal right to request.

A pointed example would be a telecommuter caring for an ill domestic partner. The role of flexible work in such a situation is useful research data, but it is not information that management or the personnel office should have. Moreover, by respecting employee privacy, evaluators will be able gather more information. Academic researchers are themselves bound by very strict rules governing the study of human subjects.

The recording of inappropriate information about employees by a program may also interfere with protocols controlling how their performance is evaluated. Telecommuting programs usually prohibit management from penalizing an employee for not being a good telecommuter. If working from home or a remote work center causes a deterioration in performance, the telecommuter returns to the office; personnel records do not reflect this change in work arrangement, even though they may reflect the performance problems that developed as a result. Management is urged in training sessions to look out for problems caused by flexible work arrangements and to terminate flexible arrangements if they affect performance. However, evaluators may be interested in the drop-out rate among flexible workers and reasons for it. Thus, there will be personnel information collected for evaluation purposes which is not appropriately part of a personnel folder.

References and Notes*

Chapter 1: Working in a Changing World

1. Qvortrup, p. 134.
2. May, p. 614.
3. Di Martino, p. 536.
4. Garrison, p. 242.
5. Ibid., p. 242–243.
6. Mokhtarian, Discussion Notes, p. 5.
7. Perin, p. 2–3.
8. Szabo, p. 20.
9. Flexible Work Arrangements: Establishing Options for Managers and Professionals, p. 2.
10. Sommer, p. 31.
11. Szabo, p. 20.
12. Mokhtarian and Salomon, p. 14 ff.
13. Hall, p. 24.
14. Unte Reader, p. 73, quoting *Parenting*, December, 1992.
15. Zedeck, p. 240.
16. Hey, p. 35.
17. Harpaz p. 90.
18. Ibid. p. 91.
19. Ibid. p. 90.
20. Galinksy, p. 13.
21. Harpaz, Ibid.
22. Grant, p. 46.
23. Grant, *Civil Engineering*, p. 6.
24. Miller, p. 11.
25. Ibid., *Civil Engineering*.
26. Novaco.

*For complete publishing information, please see the Bibliography that follows these references.

27. *Sacramento Bee*, August 30, 1993.
28. *Los Angeles Times*, April 1, 1990.
29. Ibid.
30. Klein, p. 35.
31. Gordon, 1992, p. 3.
32. Jovanis, 171–172.
33. Pelton, p. 10–11.
34. Ibid.
35. Farmanfarmaian, p. 46.

Chapter 2: What Is Flexible Work?

1. "How Corporate America Takes Its Work Home," p. 49–58.
2. Ibid.
3. Olson, p. 130.
4. Ibid.
5. Kraut, p. 20–24.
6. "The Telecommuting Phenomenon," p. 18.
7. "Guidelines", p. 1.
8. Stulgaitis.
9. Samuels.
10. "Workplace Flexibility: A Strategy for Doing Business," p. 19.
11. There is a large disparity between the percentage of organizations with flexible work policies and the percentage of their employees who actually make use of those policies. Many high-end estimates of these practices may be measuring more lip service than action.
12. Tober, p. 70–74.
13. Salomon, p. 15–28.
14. In Europe, remote work when it applies information technologies is called telework.
15. Koblenz, p. 34.
16. "Evaluation Report," p. III-48.
17. "New Evidence Supports Telecommuting," p. 59.
18. Nilles, "Concepts of Telecommuting," p. 7.
19. Bagley, p. 4-17, 4-18.
20. Elling, p. 239–249.
21. Di Martino, p. 533.
22. Morant, p. 10.
23. Qvortrup, p. 132.
24. Bagley, 4-2.
25. Olmstead, p. 260–261.
26. Lopez, p. 1157–58.
27. "The Telecommuting Phenomenon," p. 27.
28. "The Telecommuting Phenomenon," p. B-4.
29. Ibid.

30. "Satellite Work Centers," p. 1.
31. Gann, p. 476–478.
32. Ibid.
33. Spinks, p. 356.
34. Gann, Ibid.
35. Bagley, p. 3-41–3-44.
36. Bagley, p. 3-44, quoting Casey.
37. Ibid.
38. "The Telecommuting Phenomena," p. 13.
39. Seymour, p. 94–96.
40. Starfire.
41. "Satellite Work Centers," p. 1.
42. "Telecommuting Advisory Group."
43. Di Martino, p. 533.
44. "Evaluation Report", p. I-9.
45. Link Resources, February 28, 1992 Press Release, p. 4.
46. Heenan, p. 30.
47. Ibid.
48. "Make Way for Yiffies," p. 4.
49. Ibid.
50. Rothman.
51. "Satellite Work Centers," p. 2.
52. Gann, p. 473 ff.
53. Ibid.
54. Sahlberg, p. 195–96.
55. Qvortrup, p. 136.
56. Nilles, Concepts of Telecommuting, p. 301.
57. Pacific Bell Management," p. 1.

Chapter 3: Flexible Work for a Diverse Work Force

1. Klein, p. 31.
2. Flexible Work Arrangements: Establishing Options for Managers and Professionals, Executive Summary, p. ii.
3. Ibid.
4. Buhler, p. 17.
5. Tazelaar, p. 155 ff.
6. "Satellite Work Centers," p. 6.
7. Ibid.
8. Kovach, p. 52.
9. Nollen, p. 25.
10. Klein, p. 31.
11. Kovach, Ibid.
12. Werther, p. 42.
13. Stoner, p. 7.

14. Kovach, Ibid.
15. Nollen, p. 25.
16. Ibid.
17. Kovach, Ibid.
18. Nollen, Ibid.
19. Shinn, p. 32.
20. Nollen, p. 27.
21. Solomon, p. 22.
22. Ralston, p. 46.
23. Galinsky, p. 60.
24. Lefkovich, p. 103 (citing *Business and Health*, May 1991).
25. Ibid., (citing National Council on Aging).
26. Ibid.
27. Galinsky, p. 61.
28. Nollen, p. 28.
29. City of Toronto, p. 4.
30. Ibid., p. 5.
31. Ibid., p. 4.
32. USA Today, p. 37.
33. Galinksy, p. 61.
34. Shin, p. 32.
35. City of Toronto, p. 3.
36. Ibid.
37. Quoted from *American Demographics*, December, 1991, in *Unte Reader*, p. 63.
38. Zedeck, p. 248.
39. Ibid.
40. Ibid.
41. Galinsky, p. 23.
42. Zedeck, p. 244.
43. Rothberg, p. 104–106.
44. Hall, p. 28.
45. Zedeck, p. 244.
46. Hall, p. 24.
47. Stoner, p. 11.
48. Ibid.
49. Hardie, p. 10.
50. Hamilton, Carroll p. 92.
51. Stoner, p. 12.
52. Zedeck, p. 244.
53. Ibid.
54. Nollen, p. 26.
55. Hardie, p. 7.
56. Christensen, p. 17–23, 1987.
57. Ibid.
58. Goncharolff.

59. Metzger, p. 101–111.
60. Risman, p. 71–75.
61. Hamilton, C, p. 91–101.
62. Christensen, Ibid.
63. Farmanfarmaian, p. 46–52.
64. Newman p. 41.
65. "The Telecommuting Phenomenon," p. 20.
66. Risman, Ibid.
67. "Telecommuting: Staying Away in Droves," p. 88.
68. Risman, Ibid.
69. Newman, p. 41.
70. Farmanfarmaian p. 48.
71. Knobelsdorff.
72. Christensen, Ibid.
73. Kraut, p. 34.
74. Risman, Ibid.
75. Christensen, Ibid.
76. Kraut, p. 20–24.
77. Kovach, p. 53.
78. Christensen, Ibid.
79. Fleming, p. 148–150.
80. Christensen.
81. Kraut, Ibid.
82. Zedeck, p. 244.
83. Hall, p. 25.
84. Ibid.
85. "Satellite Work Centers," p. 7.
86. Hewlett, p. 5.
87. JALA Associates, "The Home Telecommuter."
88. Zedeck, Ibid.
89. Nollen, p. 27.
90. Ibid.

Chapter 4: The Benefits of Flexible Work

1. Personal Computer Week, March 1, 1988, quoted in "Evaluation Report," p. III-13.
2. McKeever, p. 2.
3. Hamilton, p. 93.
4. Schwartz, p. 8–9.
5. Guiley, p. 27–29.
6. Anonymous remarks at "Workshop."
7. Sahlberg, p. 197.
8. Di Martino, p. 531-2.
9. Ibid.

10. Hughson, p. 315–324.
11. "Evaluation Report," III-17–18.
12. Tyler, p. 18–19.
13. Bailyn, p. 464.
14. Misutka, p. 74.
15. Flexible Work Arrangements: Establishing Options for Managers and Professions, p. 89.
16. Gordon, 1986, p. 28–30.
17. Overbaugh.
18. Galant, p. 158.
19. Dalton, p. 371.
20. Ibid.
21. Ibid., p. 381.
22. "The Telecommuting Phenomenon," p. 27.
23. Reichert, p. 17.
24. Ibid.
25. "Flextime Workshop Video."
26. McGuire, p. 8.
27. Toledano.
28. Department of Transportation National Workshop on Telecommuting Issues and Impacts, Notes of 5/27/1992–5/28/1992, p. 6.
29. Fleming, 1988, p. 148–150.
30. Kelly, (2), p. 20–23.
31. Hamilton, p. 93.
32. City of Toronto, p. 14.
33. Farmanfarmaian, p. 46.
34. Nilles, Concepts of Telecommuting, p. 306.
35. Uchida, p. 9–11.
36. Nilles, Ibid.
37. Thomas, p. 43–45.
38. Thomas, Ibid.
39. McGuire, p. 8.
40. Zimmermann, p. 54.
41. Benham, pg 36.
42. "The Telecommuting Phenomenon," Ibid.
43. City of Toronto, Ibid.
44. Miller, p. 10.
45. Department of Transportation National Workshop on Telecommuting Issues and Impacts, Notes of 5/27/1992–5/28/1992, p. 9.
46. Bennett, p. 4–5.
47. "Telecommuting Advisory Group," p. 5.
48. Nilles.
49. Comment from Lis Fleming publications.
50. Pucher, p. 509.
51. Proskauer, p. 4 ff.
52. Ibid.

53. Jovanis, p. 76.
54. Pucher, p. 509.
55. Mokhtarian, 1990. p. 231–242.
56. "The Telecommuting Phenomenon," p. 5.
57. New teleconferencing technologies, known as Codecs, are able to use readily available, low cost telecommunication services to transmit images; these may make teleconferencing a more widely diffused technology.
58. Salomon.
59. Willard.
60. "New Evidence Supports Telecommuting."
61. Hamer, p. 11.
62. "Flextime Workshop Video", p. 2.
63. Stulgaitis, p. 2.
64. Mokhtarian, Ibid. p. 240.
65. "The Telecommuting Phenomenon," p. 35.
66. Nilles, Transportation Research, p. 303.

Chapter 5: Challenges to Flexible Work

1. Di Martino, p. 55.
2. Perin, p. 245.
3. Flexible Work Schedules, p. 3.
4. Perin, Ibid.
4a Shinn, p. 34.
4b Nollen, p. 29.
5. Workplace Flexibility, p. 7.
6. Risman p. 73.
7. Ibid.
8. City of Toronto, p. 16.
9. Flexible Work Arrangements: Establishing Options for Managers and Professionals, p. 12–14.
10. Nilles, 1988, p. 306.
11. McGee, p. 61.
12. Perin, p. 256 ff.
13. Ibid.
14. Ibid.
15. Ibid.
16. Home Truths About Teleworking, p. 48.
17. Risman, Ibid.
18. "Telecommuting Advisory Group," p. 17.
19. "Evaluation Report," IV-3, IV-4.
20. "Evaluation Report," IV-11.
21. Kraut, p. 20–24.
22. Solomon, p. 22.
23. Christensen, p. 23.

24. Buftam, p. 69.
25. Hamilton, p. 93.
26. "The Telecommuting Phenomenon," p. 21.
27. Christensen p. 18.
28. Hamilton, Ibid.
29. Hamilton, Ibid.
30. Knobelsdorff, p. 18.
31. "Evaluation Report," III-26.
32. "The Telecommuting Phenomenon," p. 21.
33. Guiley, p. 28.
34. Harz p. 10.
35. Metzger p. 107–108.
36. "The Telecommuting Phenomenon," p. 20.
37. Sharp, p. 84–85.
38. McKeever, p. 4.
39. Olson p. 130.
40. Ibid.
41. Bell, p. 9 ff.
42. Stackel, p. 189–197.
43. Christensen, Ibid.
44. Di Martino, p. 539.
45. Stackel, Ibid.
46. Di Martino, Ibid.
47. Ibid.
48. Elling.
49. Among industrial societies, the use of contingent workers became so common that the German trade union movement coined a term, *Kapovaz (Kapazitat-sorientierte Variable Arbeitszeit*, working hours varied on the basis of need or capacity), for the practice. Menkus.
50. Rothberg.
51. Information provided by the Telecommunications Department.
52. Rothman, p. 1(B).
53. Harper's Magazine, November 1992, pg 20.
54. Benhamp, p. 35.
55. Rothman, p. 2(B).
56. Stackel, p. 191.
57. Hartman, p. 7.
58. Rothberg, p. 104.
59. "Telecommuting Workshop."
60. "Bay Area Commuters," p. 4.
61. Dalton, p. 384–5.
62. Hamilton.
63. "Bay Area Commuters," p. 5.
64. "The Telecommuting Phenomenon," p. 24.
65. Nilles, Ibid.
66. Guiley, Ibid.

67. Hamilton p. 94.
68. Rothman, p. 2(B).
69. Solomon, p. 19 ff.
70. Elling 246.
71. Ibid.
72. Rothman, Ibid.
73. Rothberg, p. 105.
74. "Labor and Management."
75. Hardie, p. 10–11.
76. Newman p. 42.
77. Starfire.
78. Guiley p. 29.
79. Benham p. 34.
80. Hardie, p. 6.
81. Christensen, 1990. p. 92.
82. Farmanfarmaian p. 52.
83. Bailey, p. 468–469.
84. Jovanis, p. 181.
85. Christensen, p. 94.
86. Flexible Work Arrangements: Establishing Options for Managers and Professionals, p. 13.
87. Farmanfarmaian, Ibid.

Chapter 6: The Selection and Management of Flexible Workers

1. "Evaluation Report," p. II-3–5.
2. "The Telecommuting Phenomenon," posed by Mark Kempe, a Project Manager with the Interactive Systems Corporation, pg 7.
3. "The Telecommuting Phenomenon," p. 5–7.
4. "The Telecommuting Phenomenon," p. 37, #48.
5. Family and Work, p. 25 ff.
6. The National Survey of Salary, Staffing, and Professional Practice Patterns in Ambulatory Oncology Clinics, p. 17.
7. Christensen, 1987, p. 21.
8. Newman, p. 43.
9. "Telecommuting Advisory Group," p. 23.
10. Guiley, p. 28.
11. Hamilton, p. 95.
12. Newman, p. 40.
13. Risman, p. 73.
14. Sharp. p. 61 ff.
15. Farmanfarmaian, p. 48–50.
16. JALA Associates, "The Home Telecommuter."
17. Conner, p. 87.

18. Kelly, 1986, p. 22.
19. Farmanfarmaian, p. 48–50.
20. Source not for attribution.
21. Guiley p. 28.
22. Nilles, p. 305.
23. Metzger, p. 105.
24. Regenye, p. 16–17.
25. Christensen, 1987, p. 23.
26. McGee p. 60.
27. "Telecommuting Advisory Group," p. 13.
28. McGee, 60–61.
29. "Guidelines," p. 7.
30. Microytics, Inc., (c) 1988.
31. Perin, p. 23.
32. Unte Reader, p. 64.
33. Bailyn, p. 470.
34. Perin, p. 23–24.
35. Grant, p. 13–15.
36. Risman p. 74.
37. Seymour, 1986. p. 95–96.
38. Solomon p. 18.
39. Fleming p. 148.
40. Hardie, p. 9.
41. "Telecommuting Workshop."
42. Risman, Ibid.
43. Ibid.
44. Elling, p. 243.
45. "The Telecommuting Phenomenon," p. 20.
46. Galinsky, p. 45–46.
47. Starfire.
48. Ibid.
49. Nilles, p. 36.
50. Standworth, p. 52.
51. Samuels.
52. "Evaluation Report," p. III-19.
53. "Adventures in Telecommuting."
54. "Telecommuting Workshop."
55. Kraut, p. 26.
56. Hamilton, p. 96.
57. Kraut, Ibid.
58. Goodrich, p. 34.
59. "Telecommuting Workshop."
60. Ibid.
61. Di Martino, p. 543.
62. Grant, p. 45.
63. Ibid., p. 12.

64. Ibid.
65. Seymour, John, p. 46.
66. "Evaluation Report", B-2.

Chapter 7: The Technologies of Flexible Work

1. Benham, p. 34.
2. Kelly, p. 28.
3. Cross, p. 31.
4. Risman, p. 72.
5. Raths, p. 51, 53.
6. Seymour, John, p. 44.
7. *Information Technology in the Service Society*, p. 254.
8. On the other hand, perhaps the distribution of information is also allowing other employees to become decision makers and increasing the efficiency and degree of delegation. Then, the loss in one's productivity may be more than balanced by the gain in product from other employees.
9. Friedman, p. 25 ff.
10. Grubb, p. 278.
11. Survey of 300 administrative workers comparing the use of facsimile to interdepartmental mail conducted by the author at the University of California, Davis, in 1990.
12. Spinks, p. 347.
13. Benham, p. 34.
14. "Evaluation Report," p. III-11.
15. "Telecommuting: Staying Away in Droves."
16. General Office of Accounting, 1990.
17. Romei, p. 1.
18. Grant, p. 39–40.
19. Grubb, p. 278.

Part II: Implementing Flexible Work

1. "Flexibility: Compelling Strategies for a Competitive Workplace," p. 4. Du Pont's survey of 4000 workers in 1988, according to Faith Wohl, director of the company's "work force parenting" division: "This was mainly a survey of white male workers."
2. "How Corporate America Takes Its Work Home, Part I", p. 53.
3. "Evaluation Report", p. III-13–29.
4. "The Telecommuting Phenomenon," p. 27–35.
5. Telecommuting Advisory Group," p. 18.
6. Wagel, p. 14–15.
7. "Evaluation Report", p. III-8.
8. Ibid.
9. "Telecommuting Advisory Group," p. 4–5.

10. According to Flextime Workshop Video.
11. Asynchronous messages are sent and received at different times; hence, one might send electronic mail at 7 A.M. to a co-worker who will receive it several hours later.
12. "*Bay Area Commuters*," p. 6.
13. "*The Telecommuting Phenomenon*," p. 26.
14. "*How Corporate America Takes Its Work Home*," p. 48.
15. "Implementation Plan," p. 14.
16. Flemming, p. 149.
17. "The Telecommuting Phenomenon," p. 2–3.
18. "Implementation Plan," p. 15.
19. Ibid.
20. "Implementation Plan," Ibid.
21. Cook, p. 1(B).
22. Hamilton, p. 94.
23. "Implementation Plan," unnumbered second page of "Telecommuter's Agreement."
24. "The Telecommuting Phenomenon," p. 25.
25. JALA Associates, "The Home Telecommuter," p. 11.
26. "Guidelines", p. 12.
27. "Implementation Plan", Page 2 of Appendix I, "Telecommuter's Agreement."
28. JALA Associates, "Worksheet."
29. Wagel, Ibid.
30. Holtom, p. 56.
31. Agreement contents adapted from "Implementation Plan," Nilles, "Guidelines," "Telecommuting Advisory Group," Pacific Bell Management," "The Telecommuting Phenomenon."
32. Pacific Bell Management", p. 2.
33. Hardie, p. 5.
34. JALA Associates, "The Home Telecommuter," p. 13.
35. Stulgaitis, "Staggered Work Hours."
36. JALA Associates, "The Home Telecommuter."
37. Adapted from JALA Associates, "The Home Telecommuter."
38. Fortin, p. 23.
39. "The Telecommuting Phenomenon."
40. "Implementation Plan," p. 16.
41. "Telecommuting Advisory Group," p. 34.
42. The citations for these elements duplicate those referenced in the management elements above.
43. Tzelaar, p. 155 ff.
44. "Evaluation Report," IV-8.
45. See, for example, the Los Angeles County Telecommuting Handbook and the California State Department of Transportation Guide to Telecommuting, Sacramento, California.
46. For managers who will be flexible workers themselves, the participant ele-

ments are introduced in a special section. It is necessary to have separate discussions for departmental management and other participants. Experience shows that important issues do not otherwise surface.

47. Newman, p. 43.
48. McGee p. 61.
49. Bulkeley.
50. JALA Associates, "Worksheet, State of California Telecommuting Pilot."
51. Ibid.
52. "Implementation Plan," Ibid.
53. Guiley, p. 28.
54. Hamilton, p. 91–101.
55. Newman, p. 43.
56. Hamilton, Hildebrand, "Evaluation Report," Hardie, "The Telecommuting Phenomenon," Grubb, "Telecommuting: An Alternate Route."
57. "Evaluation Report."
58. JALA Associates, "Worksheet, State of California Telecommuting Pilot."
59. "Evaluation Report," III-12.
60. Misutka, p. 74.
61. General issues frequently identified by academic researchers as possible topics of study include: managing transportation demand/commuter trip reduction; space management benefits; effects on family life and family members; productivity; work discipline (absenteeism, tardiness); differences in perspectives of participants, supervisors, and co-workers, family members; morale; effects of formal and informal telecommuting arrangements on management goals; technological experiences; clerical support issues; affects of flexible work on employment related stress, sick leave, and wellness.
62. Evaluation within an organization is not value-free. The values that define whether results are positive or negative cannot be applied by scientists or consultants, but only by the organization.

Bibliography

"Adventures in Telecommuting: Getting Ready for the '90s," *On Achieving Excellence*, January, 1990, 4.

"A Paper on the Integration of Work and Family Responsibilities," City of Toronto [Canada], November 25, 1991, 2–19.

Akst, Daniel. "Telecommuting Center," Los Angeles Times, July 6, 1986.

Alexander, Michael. "Travel-free commuting," *Nation's Business*, December, 1990, 33–37.

Allen, Roland Y. "Telecommuting," Memorandum dated 16 June 1989. University of California at Davis, Business and Finance Office.

Anapol, Lynda. "High Tech Brightens Telecommuting Future," *Telephone Engineer & Management*, Vol. 90, Number 6, March 15, 1986, 74–76.

Ansley, Mary Holm. "Homing Instinct," *Listener and TV Times*, New Zealand, July 29, 1991, 34–36.

Antonoff, Michael. "The Push for Telecommuting," *Personal Computing*, Vol. 9(7), July 1985, 82–92.

Atkinson, William. "Telecommuter Blues," *Management World*, Vol. 14(10), November 1985, 44–45.

Bagley, Michael, Mannering, Jill S., Mokhtarian, Patricia L. "Telecommuting Centers and Related Concepts," Institute of Transportation Studies, University of California, Davis. 1994.

Bailey, Dori Sera, Foley, Jill. "Pacific Bell Works Long Distance," *HR Magazine*, August, 1990, 50–52.

Baily, Martin Neil. "What has happened to productivity growth?" *Science*, October 24, 1986, 443–449.

Bailyn, Lotte. "Freeing work from the constraints of location and time," *New Technology, Work and Employment*, Vol. 3(2), 1988, 143–152.

Bailyn, Lotte. "Toward the Perfect Workplace?" *Communications of the ACM*, Vol. 32(4), 1989, p. 460–471.

Barbas, Antonios N. "Telecommunications/Transportation Tradeoffs: Telecommuting Implications in a University Setting." Doctoral Dissertation. Amherst: University of Massachusetts, 1988.

"Bay Area Commuters Let Their Fingers Do the Walking," Telecommunity, November/December, 1989. Los Angeles: Southern California Association of Governments.

214

Bell, Robert A., Roloff, Michael E., Van Camp, Karen, Karol, Susan H. "Is it Lonely At the Top?: Career Success and Personal Relationships," *Journal of Communication*, Vol. 40(1), Winter 1990, 9 ff.

Benham, Barbara Tzivanis. "Telecommuting: There's No Place Like Home," *Best's Review (Life/Health)*, Vol. 89(1) May 1988, 32–38.

Bennett, Anna K. "After the quake: The Loma Prieta earthquake and employer-based transportation programs," *ITS Review*, Vol. 14(2), 1991, 4–6.

Blake, Virgil L. P., Surprenant, Thomas T. *The Information Society*, Vol. 7, 1990, 233–244.

Brown, Abby. "The Flexible Workforce—What Part-time Professionals Think," *Personnel Administrator*, August, 1986, 33–39.

Buffam, Bill. "Telecommuting on the ISDN Highway." Network World, Vol. 6(38) September 25, 1989, 65–70.

Buhler, Patricia M. "Hiring the Disabled the Solution to our Problem." *Supervision*, June, 1991, 17–19.

Bulkeley, William. M. "Gearing Up," *Wall Street Journal*, June 4, 1990.

"Can Telecommunications Help Solve America's Transportation Problems?" A multiclient study by Arthur D. Little, Inc., February, 1991, Cambridge, Massachusetts.

Christensen, Kathleen. "A Hard Day's Work In the Electronic Cottage," *Across the Board*, April, 1987, 17–23.

Christensen, Kathleen. "Remote Control," *PC Computing*, February, 1990, 90–94.

Christensen, Kathleen. "Telecommuting: Managing a Long-Distance Work Force," *Small Business Reports*, Vol. 13(8), October 1988, 64–66.

"Complying with the Employee Commute Options Program," published by Proskauer Rose Goetz & Mendelsohn, Personnel Consultants, January, 1994.

Conner, Connie Clemmons. "The Effect of Management Style on Manager's Satisfaction With Telecommuting," Doctoral Dissertation, Knoxville: The University of Tennessee, 1986.

Cook, Frank. "Homework: Insuring The At-Home Office," *San Diego Daily Transcript*, August 1, 1991, 1(B).

Coulson-Thomas, Colin. "IT and New Forms of Organisation for Knowledge Workers: Opportunity and Implementation," *Employee Relations*, Vol. 13(4), 1991, 22–32.

Crossen, Cynthia. "Home," *Wall Street Journal*, June 4, 1990.

Cross, Thomas. "Communications Software: Telecommuting Makes Information a Movable Feast," *Computerworld*, Vol. 21(31), August 3, 1987.

Dalton, Dan R., Mesch, Debra J. "The Impact of Flexible Scheduling on Employee Attendance," *Administrative Science Quarterly*, Vol. 35, 1990, 370–387.

Digilio, Alice. "Woodbridge Students Cash In on Traffic Idea," *Washington Post*, May 16, 1990.

Di Martino, Vittorio, Wirth, Linda. "Telework: A New Way of Working and Living," *International Labour Review*, Vol 129(5), 1990, 529–555.

Durkin, Tom. "Telecommuters Dodge a Multitude of Barriers by Working at Home," *Sacramento Business Journal*, March 5, 1990.

"Elder Care," *USA Today*, July 19, 1994, 37.

Elling, Monica. "Remote Work/Telecommuting—A Means of Enhancing the Quality of Life, or Just Another Method of Making Business More Brisk?" *Economic and Industrial Democracy*, Vol. 6 (1985), 239–249.

"Executive Summary, Midterm Report on State of California Telecommuting Pilot," Sacramento: State of California, October 10, 1989, 1–4.

Farmanfarmaian, Roxane. "A Manager's Guide to Making Telecommuting Succeed," *Working Woman*, February, 1989, 46–52.

Fleming, Lis and Dave. "Telecommuting and Urban Planning," Undated monograph.

Flemming, David. "A Design for Telecommuting," *Personal Computing*, Vol. 12(10), October 1988, 148–150.

"Flexibility: Compelling Strategies for a Competitive Workplace," published by New Ways to Work, Inc., in partnership with the Du Pont Corporation, San Francisco, California, 1991.

"Flexible Work Arrangements: Establishing Options for Managers and Professionals," published by Catalyst, Inc., New York, New York, 1989.

"Flexible Work Schedules," *Supervision*, June, 1990, 3–4.

"Flextime Workshop Video," Public Private Transportation Network, Silver Springs, Maryland.

Fortin, Karen A., Dennis-Escoffier, Shirley. "Telecommuting Adds a New Dimension to Office in the Home: Steps to Qualify for a Business Deduction," *Woman CPA*, Vol. 48(4), October 1986, 21–25.

Freedman, David H. "Culture of Urgency," *Forbes ASAP*, September 13, 1993, 25–28.

Fuller, Marsha. "The Federal Alternative Work Center," Memorandum published by the City of Hagerstown, Maryland. (undated)

Fusco, Mary Ann Castronovo. "Employment Relations Programs," *Employment Relations Today*, Autumn, 1990.

Galant, Debbie. "Far from the madding crowd," *Institutional Investors*, December, 1991, 157–158.

Galinsky, Ellen, Bond, James T., Friedman, Dana E. *The Changing Workforce*, New York: Families and Work Institute, 1993.

Gann, David M. "Buildings for the Japanese Information Economy," *Futures*, June, 1991, 469–481.

Garrison, William L., Deakin, Elizabeth. "Travel, Work, and Telecommunications: A View of the Electronics Revolution and Its Potential Impacts," *Transportation Research A*, Vol. 22A(4), 1988, 239–245.

Gite, Lloyd. "The home-based executive," *Black Enterprise*, January, 1991, 63–65.

Goates, Joseph F., Jarratt, Jennifer, Mahaffie, John B. "Future Work," *The Futurist*, May/June, 1991, 10–19.

Goncharolff, Katya. "Telecommuters Say There's No Workplace Like Home," *The New York Times*, Business Section, March 24, 1985.

Goodrich, Jonathan N. "Telecommuting in America," *Business Horizons*, July/August, 1990, 31–36.

Gordon, Gil E. "Insurers In Telecommuting Vanguard," *National Underwriter* (Property and Casualty/Employee Benefits), February 16, 1987, page 18–19, 55.

Gordon, Gil E. "Microcomputers Spur Interest in Telecommuting," *Computerworld*, Vol. 19(17) April 29, 1985.

Gordon, Gil E. "Telecommuting: Domestic Work," *Network World*, Vol. 3(14) June 9, 1986, 28–30.

Gordon, Gil E. "Telecommuting: Emphasizing Work, Not the Work Place," *Journal of Accounting & EDP*, Vol. 2(3), Fall 1986, 34–41.

Gordon, Gil E. "Telecommuting: Planning for a New Work Environment," *Journal of Information Systems Management*, Vol. 3(3), Summer 1986, 37–44.

Gordon, Gil E. "Telecommuting Stretches Nets Beyond Office Setting," *Computerworld*, Vol. 19(43) October 28, 1985, 78–100.

Gordon, Gil. "Telecommuting Offers New Area for Greater Teleconferencing Growth," *Communications News*, February 1985, 81.

Gordon, Gil. "Telework Troubles, Traumas, and Triumphs: Confessions from the Telework Planners Around the Pacific Rim," Speech to the Pacific Telecommunications Council, January 15, 1992.

Gordon, Gill. "Telecommuting Review," published by Gil Gordon Associates, June, 1991.

Gordon, Gill. "Telecommuting Review," published by Gil Gordon Associates, January, 1992.

Gordon, Gill. "Telecommuting Review," published by Gil Gordon Associates, August, 1992.

Grant, Albert A. "Telecommuting: Civil Engineering Opportunity," *Civil Engineering*, p. 6. (undated)

Grant, K. A., Hoffman, D., Cukier, W. "A Study of the Concepts of Telework and Telecommuting in the National Capital Region," Stevenson Kellogg Ernst & Whinney, Management Consultants, a project report prepared for the National Capital Commission, Government of Canada, Ottawa, February, 1987.

Grevstad, Eric. "Telecommuter: Laptop Meets Desktop," *Tele: The Communications Magazine for Business*, Vol. 1(4) January [year missing], 68–71.

Grubb, William F. X. "The Dual Office in Our Future," *Personal Computing*, October, 1988, 278.

"Guidelines for Pilot Flexible Workplace Arrangements," Washington, D.C.: Presidents Council on Management Improvement, Human Resources Committee, January, 1990.

Guiley, Rosemary. "When Your Employees Work From Home. How you can develop and manage a telecommuting program, while avoiding many of its pitfalls," *Working Woman*, March, 1985, 27–29.

"Hagerstown-to-D.C. Commuters Could Work Here From There," *The Washington Post*, December 29, 1991, p. B1.

Hall, Douglas T. "Moving Beyond the Mommy Track: An Organization Change Approach," *Personnel*, December, 1989, 23–29.

Hamer, Mike. "Home work clears air," *New Scientist*, October 5, 1991, 11.

Hamer, Rebecca, Kroes, Eric, Van Ooststroom, Harry. "Teleworking in the Netherlands: An Evaluation of Changes in Travel Behaviour," *Transportation*, Vol. 18, 1991, 362–382.

Hamilton, Brodie. "Staggered Work Hours—Implementation Approach," Unpublished memorandum. Davis: University of California at Davis, Department of Transportation and Parking Services, June, 1989.

Hamilton, Carol-Ann. "Telecommuting," *Personnel Journal*, April, 1987, 91–101.

Hardie, John. L. "Telecommuting—A Possible Work Option for The University of California, Davis." Davis: Draft memorandum, University of California at Davis, September 13, 1989.

Harpaz, Itzhak. "The Importance of Work Goals: An International Perspective," *Journal of International Business Studies*, First Quarter, 1990, 75–93.

Hartman, Sally Kirby. "The Computer Commuter," *Virginia Business*, September, 1990, 7 ff.

Harz, Nan S. "Telecommuting—There's No Place Like Home," *Data Management*, June, 1985, 10–11.

Heenan, David A. "New corporate frontiers," *Across the Board*, November, 1991, 29–34.

Hewlett, Sylvia Ann. "It's time we put children first," *Parade Magazine*, July 17, 1994, 4–5.

Hey, Kenneth R. "Business as usual? Forget it," *Across the Board*, January/February, 1992, 30–25.

Hildebrand, Carol. "Who Bears the Burden?" *PCs & Workstations*, [Date unknown].

Holtom, Robert B. "There's No Workplace Like Home," *Best's Review*, [Date unknown], 55–56.

"How Corporate America Takes its Work Home, Part I," *Modern Office Technology*, July 1989, 49–58.

"How Corporate American Takes Its Work Home, Part II," *Modern Office Technology*, August, 1989, 45–50.

"How Employees Benefit from Telecommuting," published by the County of Riverside, Telecommuting Work Center, Riverside, California. (undated)

"How to Implement an Alternate Work Schedule Program," published by the Maricopa County Travel Reduction Program, Maricopa County, Arizona. (undated)

Hughson, Terri L., Goodman, Paul S. "Telecommuting: Corporate Practices and Benefits," *National Productivity Review*, Autumn, 1986, 315–322.

Huws, Ursula. "Telework: Projections," Futures, January/February, 1991, 19–31.

"Inter-City Commute Transit Service," Memorandum from the Transportation Administrative Advisory Committee to Chancellor Hullar, Vice Chancellor Sullivan. Davis: University of California at Davis, Business and Finance Office, 1990.

"IRS Clarifies Home-Office Rules," Linda Stern, *The San Diego Union*, C-3 (undated).

Jack, Andrew. "Home is Where the Terminal Is." *London Times*, July 31, 1991.

JALA Associates. "The Home Telecommuter," Noted as Version 1.6, [Date unknown].

JALA Associates. "Worksheet 5.2.3.1" [Page and date unknown].

JALA Associates, "Worksheet, State of California Telecommuting Pilot."

"Job Stress Claims Increase Dramatically in California," *The Los Angeles Times*, April 1, 1990.

Jovanis, Paul P. "Telecommunications and Alternative Work Schedules: Options for Managing Transit Travel Demand," *Urban Affairs Quarterly*, Vol. 19(2), 1983, 167–189.

Katz, Adolph I. "The Management, Control, and Evaluation of a Telecommuting Project: A Case Study," *Information & Management (Netherlands)*, Vol. 13(4) November 1987, 179–190.

Kelley, Marcia M. "Telecommuting: The Next Computer Revolution," *Small Business Report*, Vol. 11(4), April 1986.

Kelly, Marcia. "The Next Workplace Revolution: Telecommuting," *Supervisory Management*, October, 1985, 2–7.

Kelly, Marcia M. "Telecommuting: The Next Workplace Revolution," *Information Strategy: The Executive's Journal*, Vol. 2(2) Winter 1986, 20–23.

Kelly, Marcia M. "The Work at Home Revolution," *The Futurist*, November-December 1988, 28–32.

Kinsman, Francis. "Telecommuting: An Idea Whose Time Has Come," *Accountancy (UK)*, Vol. 104(1154) October 1989, 166–169.

Klein, Easy. "Tomorrow's Work Force," *D&B Reports*, January/February, 1990, 33–35.

Knobelsdorff, Elizabeth. "Telecommuting Reality Sets In," *Christian Science Monitor*, [Page and date unknown].

Koblenz, Jay. "Telecommuting—Traveling to Work Via Your Computer," *Black Enterprise*, November 1986, 34.

Komarnitsky, S. "Commuters keep close to home with telework centers," *The North Seattle Press*, August 7, 1991, 9.

Kovach, Kenneth A., Pearce, John A. II. "HR Strategic Mandates for the 1990s." *Personnel*, April, 1990, 50–55.

Kraut, Robert E. "Telecommuting: The Trade-Offs of Home Work," *Journal of Communication*, Summer, 1989, Vol 39(3).

Kuzela, Lad. "When Going to Work Means Staying Home," *Modern Office Technology*, June, 1987, 30.

"Labor and Management Take on the Politics of Telecommuting," *On Achieving Excellence*, January, 1990.

La Mountain, Fran. "Telecommuting Pilot Project Plan," TRW Defense Systems Group (internal memorandum), April, 1987. Includes Training Outline by Gil Gordon, April, 1987.

Lefkovich, Jeff L. "Business Responds to Elder Care Needs," *HR Magazine*, June, 1992.

Llana, Andres, Jr. "Your Database Hits Home with Telecommuting," *CommunicationAge*, Vol. 3(11) November 1986, 34–39.

Lopez, David A., Gray, Paul. "The Substitution of Communication for Transportation: A Case Study," *Management Science*, Vol. 23(11), July, 1977, p. 1149–1159.

"Make Way for Yiffies," *Business Digest*, Pacific Bell, November/December, 1990.

Mattis, Mary C. "New forms of flexible work arrangements for managers and professionals: myths and realities," *Human Resource Planning*, Vol. 13(2), 133–147.

May, Graham H. "The Future of the City: Issues for the 21st century," *Futures,* July/August, 1990, 607–617.

McCarthy, Mike. "Isleton plans for growth with telecommuting plan," *The Business Journal,* Sacramento, California, June 24, 1991, 45.

McGee, Lynne F. "Setting Up Work at Home," *Personnel Administrator,* December, 1988, 58–62.

McGugan, Ian. "Phoning It In: Advantages of Telecommuting," *Computing Canada,* Vol. 13(12) 22 June 11, 1987.

McGuire, Jean B., Liro, Joseph R. "Absenteeism and Flexible Work Schedules," *Public Personnel Management,* Vol. 16, No. 1 (Spring, 1987). 7–8

McKeever, Chris, Guinn, Melanie. "An Introduction To Telecommuting," Orange County Transit District Pilot Telecommuting Program, November, 1989.

McKeever, Christopher, Valez, Roberta. "Telecommuting: A review of literature and programs." Published by the Orange County Transit District, Garden Grove, California, June, 1989, 1–10.

Menkus, Belden. "Recommended Reading," *Journal of Systems Management,* May 22, 1987.

Metzger, Robert O., Von Glinow, Mary Ann. "Off Site Workers: At Home and Abroad," California Management Review, Spring 1988, 101–111.

Miller, Thomas. "Telecommuting Benefits Business with DP's Help (Part 1)," *Computerworld,* Vol. 20(7) February 17, 1986, 51–55.

Misutka, Frances. "The Workplace Takes Wing," *Canadian Business,* May, 1992, 73–77.

Mokhtarian, Patricia. "Telecommuting in the United States," Speech to the Yokohama Prefecture, Japan, September, 1992 (slide book).

Mokhtarian, Patricia L. "An Empirical Evaluation of the Travel Impacts of Teleconferencing," *Transportation Research A,* Vol. 22A(4), 1988, 283–289.

Mokhtarian, Patricia L. "Defining Telecommuting," Institute of Transportation Studies, University of California, Davis, May, 1991.

Mokhtarian, Patricia L. "Discussion Notes, 'Telecommunications, Information Systems, and Transportation,' " January 12, 1988, 67th Annual Meeting of the Transportation Research Board, Washington, D.C.

Mokhtarian, Patricia L., Salomon, Ilan. "Modeling the choice of telecommuting: setting the context," *Environment and Planning A* (in press), March, 1993.

Mokhtarian, Patricia L. "Telecommuting and travel: State of the Practice, State of the Art." *Transportation,* Vol. 18, 1991, 319–342.

Mokhtarian, Patricia L. "The Air Quality Benefits of Telecommuting," (slide book, undated)

Mokhtarian, Patricia L. "The Effectiveness of Telecommuting As A Transportation Control Measure," Institute of Transportation Studies, University of California, Davis, August, 1991.

Mokhtarian, Patricia L. "The Transportation Impacts of Telecommuting in Two San Diego Pilot Programs," Institute of Transportation Studies, University of California, Davis, October, 1991.

Mokhtarian, Patricia L. "A Typology of Relationships Between Telecommunications and Transportation," *Transportation Research, Part A*, Vol. 24A(3), 231–242.

Mokhtarian, Patricia L. "Evaluation Report—Telecommuting Pilot Project for the Southern California Association of Governments," Los Angeles: Central City Association and the Southern California Association of Governments, August, 1988.

Mokhtarian, Patricia L. "Implementation Plan—Telecommuting Pilot Project for the Southern California Association of Governments," Los Angeles: Central City Association, January, 1986.

Mokhtarian, Patricia L. "The Telecommuting Phenomenon: Overview and Evaluation," Los Angeles: Southern California Association of Governments, March, 1985.

Monant, Adrian J. "Rural Scots Use ISDN Service to Work at Home," *Communication News*, June, 1993, p. 10–11.

Moore, Steve. "Telecommuting: Today, Tomorrow or Never?" *On Communications*, Vol. 2(8) August 1985, 29–30.

Moss, Jennings J. "Plan aims to keep workers by letting them toil at home," *The Washington Post*, March 3, 1990.

Muller, Nathan J. "Telecommuting Costs Climb with Divestiture," *Telephone Engineer & Management*, Vol. 89(7) April 1, 1985, 76–84.

National Research Council. *Information Technology in the Service Society: A twenty-first century lever*. Washington: National Academy Press, 1994.

Needle, David. "Telecommuting: Off to a Slow Start," *InfoWorld*, Vol. 8(20) May 19, 1986, 43–46.

"New Evidence Supports Telecommuting," *The Futurist*, July-August, 1990, 59.

Newman, Stuart. "Telecommuters Bring the Office Home," *Management Review*, Vol. 78(12) December 1989, 40–43.

Nilles, Jack M. "Concepts of Telecommuting," Los Angeles, JALA Associates, 1988.

Nilles, Jack M. "Telecommuting and Energy Conservation: The Realities," Testimony before the California Energy Commission, May 1, 1990, Sacramento, California, Docket 89-CR-90.

Nilles, Jack M. "The Case for Telework Centers," Speech to the Minnesota Telecommuting Conference, Bloomington, Minnesota, May 15, 1991.

Nilles, Jack M. "Traffic Reduction by Telecommuting: A Status Review and Selected Bibliography." *Transportation Research A*, Vol. 22A(4), 1988, 301–317.

Nollen, Stanley D. "The Work-Family Dilemma: How HR Managers Can Help," *Personnel*, May, 1989, 25–30.

"Notes of the May 27–28, 1992, Workshop on Telecommuting Issues and Impacts," U.S. Department of Transportation, 1992.

Novaco, Raymond W., Kliewer, Wendy, Broquet, Alex. "Home Environment Consequences of Commute Travel Impedence." *American Journal of Community Psychology*, Vol. 19(6), 1991, 881–886.

Novaco, Raymond W., Stokols, Daniel, Milanesi, Louis. "Objective and Subjective Dimensions of Travel Impedance as Determinants of Commuting Stress," *American Journal of Community Psychology*, Vol. 18(2), 1990, 231–257.

Olmsted, Barney. "Flexible Work Arrangements: A Sea of Change for Managers," *Employment Relations Today*, Winter, 1991, 291–295.

Olmsted, Barney, Smith, Suzanne. "Flex for Success!" *Personnel*, June, 1989, 50–55.

Olson, Margrethe H., Tasley, Roberta. "Telecommunications and the Changing Definition of the Workplace," in *Policy Research in Telecommunications: Proceedings from the Eleventh Annual Telecommunications Policy Research Conference*, Vincent Mosco, editor. Norwood: 1984, 248 ff.

Olson, Margrethe H. "Do you Telecommute?" *Datamation*, October 15, 1985, 129–132.

"One in Five Major U.S. Firms Now Uses Telecommuting," press release of February, 1992, Link Resources Corporation, Ithaca, New York.

"Ontario Comm Center Brochure."

Overbaugh, Maggie. "Home Terminal," Memorandum dated 21 November 1989. Davis: University of California at Davis, Department of Telecommunications.

"Pacific Bell Management Telecommuting Policy," [Page and date unknown]. Printed by Pacific Bell.

Pelton, Joseph N. "Telepower: The Emerging Global Brain," *The Futurist*, September/October, 1989, 9–14.

Pendyala, Ram M., Goulias, Konstadinos G., Kitamura, Ryuichi. "Impact of Telcommuting on Spatial and Temporal Patterns of Household Travel," *Transportation*, Vol. 18, 1991, 383–409.

Perin, Constance. "The Moral Fabric of the Office: Panopticon Discourse and Schedule Flexibilities," *Research in the Sociology of Organizations*, Vol. 8, 1991, 241–268.

Peters, Tom. "*On Achieving Excellence*" (Newsletter), January, 1990, pages 4–5.

Porter, Sylvia. "Computers Link Disabled to Job World," *Los Angeles Times*, August 22, 1990, B4.

Pratt, Joanne H. "Employees' Home Offices A Hidden Asset," *Contingency Journal*, September/October, 1991 (in press).

Pucher, John. "Urban Travel Behavior as the Outcome of Public Policy: The Example of Modal-Split in Western Europe and North America," *APA Journal*, Autumn, 1988, 509–520.

"Puget Sound Telecommuting Demonstration," published by the Washington State Energy Office, Olympia, Washington, April, 1991.

"Puget Sound Telecommuting Demonstration Update 1." Seattle: Washington State Energy Office (WSEO), May, 1990.

Qvortrup, Lars. "Telework: Visions, Definitions, Realities, Barriers," final Draft of paper in press, Organization for Economic Co-operation and Development, Paris, 1992.

Ralston, David A. "How flextime eases work/family tensions," *Personnel*, August, 1990, 45–48.

Raths, David. "Taking an Alternative Route," *Infoworld*, December 10, 1990, 51–56.

Reddin, W. J. *Effective Management by Objectives*, New York: McGraw-Hill, 1971.

Regenye, Steve. "Telecommuting," *Journal of Information Management*, Vol. 6(2) Winter 1985, 15–23.

"Regulation XV: Trip Reduction/Indirect Source," published by the South Coast Air Quality Mnagement District, May 17, 1990, as Rule 1501, Los Angeles, California.

Reichert, James. "After Years of Debate, Telecommuting Is Actually Working," *Transit California*, June, 1990, 17.

Remington, Richard. "Go West, Young Woman!" *Telephony*, November 7, 1988, 30–32.

Risman, Barbara J., Tomaskovic-Devey, Donal. "The Social Construction of Technology: Microcomputers and the Organization of Work," *Business Horizons*, May-June, 1989, 71–75.

Ritter, Anne. "Dependent Care Proves Profitable," *Personnel*, March, 1990, 12–16.

Rogers, Everett M. "Diffusion of innovations: enhancing the acceptance of transportation demand management programs." Slide book of presentation to the Conference on Transportation Demand Management, Policy Implications of Recent Behavioral Research, Lake Arrowhead, California, October 12–13, 1989.

Romei, Lura K. "The Home Office: Alive and Well," *Modern Office Technology*, August, 1990, 23–26.

Rothberg, Diane S. "Part-Time Professionals: The Flexible Work Force," *Personnel Administrator*, Vol. 31(8) August 1986, 104–106 ff.

Rothman, David H. "The Computer Cottage Industry Hysteria," *Washington Post*, [Date unknown].

Rothwell, Sheila. "Flexible Working Practices," *Journal of General Management*, Vol. 11, No. 2, Winter, 1985, 74–80.

Sahlberg, Bengt. "Remote Work in the Ecotronic Society" (Short Note). *Scandinavian Housing and Planning Research*, Vol. 4, 1987, 193–198.

Salomon, Ilan, Solomon, Meira. "Telecommuting: The Employee's Perspective," *Technological Forecasting and Social Change*, Vol. 25, 15–28 (1984).

Samuels, Alisa. "Scope of Flexibility Work Schedules Seen Limited," *Los Angeles Times*, [Page and date unknown].

Sandler, Corey. "Are you a candidate for telecommuting?" *Creative Computing*, August, 1985, 26–27.

"Satellite Work Centers: A Home Office Away from Home," *Telecommunity*, January/March, 1990.

Savage, J. A. "California Smog Fuels Telecommuting Plans," *Computerworld*, May 2, 1988, 64–66.

Savage, J. A. "Taking the 'Place" out of Workplace," *Computerworld*, May 14, 1990.

Schepp, Brad. "The Best Opportunities for Telecommuters," *Home-Office Computing*, October, 1990. Page 49–51.

Schwartz, Matthew. "Telecommuting Is Finding an Insurance Niche," *National Underwriter (Life/Health/Financial Services)*, Vol. 94(7) February 12, 1990, 8–9.

Seymour, James. "The Decline of the Central Office," *PC Magazine*, October 14, 1986, 95–96.

Seymour, John. "Transportation and Economic Competitiveness," from Technology for Tomorrow's Transportation, Executive Summary, Conference Report, California Engineering Foundation, November 9–10, 1989.

Sharp, Billy Joe. "Telecommuter Personality Characteristics: A Comparison of Workers in the Home and Office," Doctoral Dissertation. Los Angeles: California School of Professional Psychology, 1988.

Shinn, Maybeth, Wong, Nora W., Simko, Patricia A., Ortiz-Torres, Blanca. "Promoting the well-being of working parents: Coping, social support, and flexible job schedules," American Journal of Community Psychology, Vol. 17(1), 1989, 31–55.

Siembab, Walter, Read, Tom. "Institutional Mobility: A Cost-effective Approach to Economic Growth and Environmental Protection," Western City, July, 1992, 4–31.

Simpson, Karl. "Review of Handbook of Management by Objectives." Personnel Psychology, [Date unknown], 680–683.

Sissine, Fred. "Telecommuting: A National Option for Conserving Oil," Congressional Research Service, Library of Congress, November 9, 1990.

Sommer, Kim L., Malins, Deborah Y. "Flexible Work Solutions," Small Business Reports, August, 1991, 29–41.

Spinks, Wendy A. "Satellite and resort offices in Japan," Transportation, Vol. 18(4), 1991, 343–363.

Stackel, Leslie. "The Flexible Work Place," Employment Relations Today, Vol. 14(2) Summer 1987, 189–197.

Starfire, Brian. "Telecommuting an Idea Awaiting Its Time," Washington Post, [Date unknown].

Stein, Todd. "Firms flex to meet employee needs." The Business Journal, Sacramento, California, July 2, 1990, 18–19.

Stoner, Charles R., Hartman, Richard I. "Family Responsibilities and Career Progress: The Good, the Bad, and the Ugly," Business Horizons, May/June 1990, 7–14.

"Study: Stress May Raise Risk of Colorectal Cancer," The Sacramento Bee, August 30, 1993.

Stulgaitis, Lisa. "Staggered Work Hours," Unpublished memorandum. Davis: University of California at Davis, Department of Transportation and Parking Services, March, 1989.

Stulgaitis, Lisa. "Survey of Staggered Work Hour Programs," Unpublished memorandum. Davis: University of California at Davis, Department of Transportation and Parking Services, October, 1990.

Sullivan, Nick. "How to Commute at the Speed of Light," Los Angeles: Newsletter of the Association for Commuter Transportation, July/August, 1990.

Szabo, Joan C. "Finding the right workers," Nation's Business, February, 1991, 16–22.

Tazelaar, Jane M. "Working At Home With Computers," Byte, March 1986, 155 ff.

"Telecommuters: The New Cottage Industry" National Underwriter (Life and Health/Financial Services), April 27, 1987, 23–27.

Telecommuting Advisory Group, State of California. "Telecommuting Work Option: Definition, Guidelines, and Policy," March, 1990 (draft). Sacramento: State of California.

"Telecommuting and Labor Relations," *Telecommunity*, November/December, 1989. Los Angeles: Southern California Association of Governments.

"Telecommuting: An Alternate Route to Work," Monograph. Seattle: Washington State Energy Office, undated.

"Telecommuting: It's Dialing for Dollars," *San Jose Mercury News*, August 4, 1991, B1.

"Telecommuting: Its Role and Value in Work and Family Programs," Bureau of National Affairs, March/April, 1992.

"Telecommuting: Staying Away in Droves," *The Economist*, April 4, 1987, 88.

"Telecommuting: The Coming 'Second Wave'," press memorandum of October, 1989, Link Resources Corporation, Ithaca, New York.

"Telecommuting Work Option," published by the State of California Telecommuting Advisory Board, June, 1991, Sacramento, California.

Telecommuting Workshop for Cities and Counties, October 3, 1990. Sponsored by the County of Los Angeles, Pacific Bell, and Commuter Transportation Services, Inc.

"Telework for Economic Development," published by the Technology Place, Management Consultants, Santa Monica, California, undated.

Terry, Susan. "Telecommuters Take a Byte out of Traffic." *Transactions* [Metropolitan Transportation Commission], December 1988/January 1989, 2–3.

"The Calculated Layoff," *Harper's Magazine*, November, 1992, 20.

"The National Survey of Salary, Staffing, and Professional Practice Patterns in Ambulatory Oncology Clinics," produced by the Oncology Nursing Press, April, 1992.

"The Potential Benefits of Telecommuting," Report of the Virginia Employment Commission, House Document No. 13, Commonwealth of Virginia, Richmond, 1991.

Thomas, Edward G. "Flexible Work Keeps Growing." *Modern Woman*, April/May, 1986, 43–45.

Tober, Pamela A. "The Emerging Flexible Workplace," *Compensation & Benefits Review*, Vol. 20(1) January/February 1988, 70–74.

Tobia, Randall L. "Telecommunications in the 1990s," *Business Horizons*, January/February, 1990, 81–86.

Toledano, Judith. "Telecommuting & Office Automation: The CPUC's Experience," *Government Technology*, [Page and date unknown].

"Transportation and Development: Trends and Choices," Published by the Puget Sound Council of Governments, Washington, December, 1988.

Trost, Cathy. "Close to you," *Wall Street Journal*, June 4, 1990.

Tyler, Geoff. "Waiting for the Telecommuter," *Management Accounting (UK)*, Vol. 67(3) March 1989, 18–19.

Uchida, Edward K. "Hawaii Telework Center Demonstration Project," Honolulu: Hawaii State Department of Transportation, March, 1990 (reprint).

"University of California and AFSCME Agreement, Clerical and Allied Services Unit, November 1, 1988–June 30, 1991." Davis: University of California at Davis.

"University of California and AFSCME Agreement, Service Unit, November 1, 1988–June 30, 1991." Davis: University of California at Davis.

Utne Reader, May/June, 1993.

Wagel, William H. "Telecommuting Arrives in the Public Sector," *Personnel*, October, 1988, 14–15.

Wakin, Edward. "Telecommuting: Today's Home Work," *Today's Office*, Vol. 20(7) December 1985, 23–28.

Weatherall, David. "Flexitime," *Management Services*, September, 1989, 36–39.

Weddle, David. "Aren't You Going To Work?" *California*, May, 1990, 63 ff.

Weiss, Julian M. "Adding vision to telecommuting." *The Futurist*, May/June, 1992, 16–18.

Index

227